C000070136

BY APPOINTMENT
TO HM THE QUEEN
MANUFACTURERS OF LAND ROVERS
AND RANGE ROVERS
LAND ROVER UK LTD., SOLIHULL

BY APPOINTMENT
TO HRH THE DUKE OF EDINBURGH
VEHICLE MANUFACTURERS
LAND ROVER UK LTD., SOLIHULL

BY APPOINTMENT
TO HM QUEEN ELIZABETH THE QUEEN MOTHER
MANUFACTURERS OF LAND ROVERS
LAND ROVER UK LTD., SOLIHULL

BY APPOINTMENT
TO HRH THE PRINCE OF WALES
VEHICLE MANUFACTURERS
LAND ROVER UK LTD., SOLIHULL

Winching in Safety

LAND ROVER LTD

(i)

The Land Rover Guide to Winching In Safety has been published for and on behalf of Land Rover UK Ltd. by The Land Rover Directory.

Written and compiled by Peter Hobson.

CONTENTS

An Introduction to Winching

A winch adds a great deal to the versatility of an off-road vehicle. This Land Rover Guide to Winching describes the various types of winch available that are approved for fitting to Land Rovers and Range Rovers, and how to use them safely.

For the benefit of those unfamiliar with winches, there are two categories of use: 'Casual' for such purposes as occasionally pulling a small boat out of harbour, or self-recovery of a disabled vehicle, and 'Heavy duty'. This category includes any number of jobs: cable laying, tree-felling and removal, putting up overhead power lines, and so on, for which the winch is likely to be in constant use. This Guide to Winching deals primarily with casual use, and is intended to advise and inform the casual user.

Before buying a winch, discuss your specific requirements with the supplier. The foremost considerations being those of safety in operation, the vehicle's ability to accept the product selected, the winch being of sufficient capacity to meet your needs and that it will not overload the vehicle and damage the chassis. Land Rover Ltd approve certain winches for fitment to Land Rovers and Range Rovers. These winches have undergone rigorous tests to ensure that they are suitable for the vehicle and are covered in the section on winches. If fitting a non-approved winch it should be borne in mind that the Land Rover Ltd warranty could well be jeopardised. In such cases where poor fitment results in distortion of the chassis frame, or the winch coming adrift from the vehicle, it should be emphasised that responsibility lies entirely with the purchaser, whose life could be put at risk in such circumstances.

1

All the winches covered in this guide have been approved by Land Rover Ltd for fitting to either the Land Rover or the Range Rover. The winches covered here are rated to pull up to a maximum of 3860kg (8500lb) which is sufficient to recover a disabled vehicle. In all cases the gross vehicle weight (GVW), or maximum weight including vehicle, passengers, fuel and luggage has been taken into account when choosing these winches. All have fitting kits for either Land Rovers or Range Rovers and can be installed by anyone with a good set of tools and reasonable engineering knowledge.

It should be noted that for convenience when ordering a new Land Rover or Range Rover, a winch can be factory-fitted. This is a service not available from most other manufacturers. The factory-fitted winch will be of approved design and suitable for its intended usage and will not, under normal operations, damage the vehicle or its chassis.

The basic definition of a winch is a machine for hoisting or hauling, using cable wound round a drum, but the applications thereof are many and varied. This winching Guide deals only with hauling applications.

Winches may be driven in one of three ways:-

        (i) Electrically.

        (ii) Mechanically.

        (iii) Hydraulically.

Electric winches, powered from the vehicle's battery, are normally of the "drum" type and generally considered to be the easiest to fit, making them the most popular for recreational or casual use.

Mechanical winches are a more complex prospect. There are two kinds, "drum" or "capstan", both of which are shaft-driven. The capstan is usually powered from the front of the engine's crankshaft, whereas the drum type, whilst sometimes driven from the same place, is more commonly connected to the power take-off point on the host vehicle's transfer box. This has the added advantage of making the primary gearbox ratios available to the winch drive. Occasionally, instead of utilising a shaft drive, a hydraulic pump will be fitted to the power take-off and the pressure generated used to power a motor in the winch. This provides the user with a versatile machine suitable for heavy duty operations.

The main factors to be considered when selecting a winch are:-

1. Intended duties i.e. casual or regular usage.

2. Maximum line pull or capacity required.

3. Availability of fitting kits and ease of installation.

4. Ease of operation for your particular application.

Naturally, as the specification is improved so the cost will rise, and this too may well be a matter for serious consideration before the ideal winch system can be identified.

There are of course 'special purpose' winches approved for fitment to the Land Rover such as the 'Plummett' and 'Fairey' (Superwinch). These winches are basically auto capstans having a facility for stowage of considerable lengths of cable, are used primarily for hauling cables through underground ducts and are used by utility services such as the Electricity Generating Board's and British Telecom.

Winching in Safety

The right winch for the job, correctly installed on the vehicle with all manufacturer's instructions having been scrupulously followed, should present no problems and provide the user with a first-class winching system. However, winches can be damaged or put out of action by careless or reckless use, overloading or poor maintenance. They can be repaired or replaced without too much pain, but not so the user, or bystanders. **The operator has a responsibility to keep the winch and its equipment in good order.**

When fitting a winch, the included literature gives advice on how to use it correctly. This must be properly studied and kept for reference. The emphasis should be on winching without danger - when in doubt, stop and re-appraise the situation and opt for personal safety.

Many winches are capable of pulling 3600kg (8,000lb) and there is now a tendency towards 4500kg (10,000lb) and 5400kg (12,000lb) models which, for self-recovery at least, are regarded as slightly over-the-top. If necessary pulling power can be doubled by introducing a pulley block, the cable routed through the pulley and back to a suitable anchor point on the vehicle. The effect is to increase pulling capacity of the winch by 2:1. So a winch rated at 3600kg (8,000lb) line-pull can effectively have 7200kg (16,000lb) line-pull. Using a pulley block in this way halves the speed of the winching operation, which can be an advantage. On an electric winch the current drawn from the battery with this configuration is also reduced by about 50 per cent. In tricky situations it is possible to use 2 pulley blocks in the line (provided sufficient anchorage points are available) for 'short-term' heavy load pulling only.

A pulley block can be a distinct advantage, and pulling another vehicle that has bottomed-out can be relatively easy on the winch. The vehicle, however, will not take unlimited strain; too much load over a long period may well twist the chassis and at best it may damage the winch mountings. Pulley blocks are a useful accessory, but only when used wisely and with great care and caution.

Cable breakages should not occur provided the cable is regularly inspected, but it is possible for the cable to be damaged and to start deteriorating after a check, underlining the need for frequent cable inspections. A cable snapping under strain can have the most frightening and serious consequences. A section has been included on care and maintenance of both wire rope and cordage and following these guide lines should forestall most cable problems.

Before tackling a winching operation, there should be a few minutes deliberation, to assess the right line of approach. The operator should look at the ground between himself and the anchor-point at the other end of the cable and question whether the winching operation is safe, or whether the cable has a clear run so that - should the cable part - the winch operator will be afforded some protection. If there is no natural cover, a coat placed over the cable may reduce the tendency for the cable to whip-lash. It may be possible to stay in the cab to operate the winch, or perhaps place another vehicle in such a way as to provide some protection. Assistants and/or spectators must stand well back, at a safe distance. A parting cable may well whip-back and can cause disfiguring and even fatal accidents. It cannot be overstated that before setting the winch drum turning it is the responsibility of the operator to ensure that no-one, repeat NO-ONE, is in any danger whatsoever. With a little thought and care, winching may be carried out safely with complete confidence.

Gloves

Steel winch cable can get into an awful mess, especially when it has been pulled out across a boggy field. It will attract anything that will stick to it, and a good pair of gloves is essential for handling it. In any winching operation gloves are vital, whether the sun is shining and the ground is dry, or the rain is bucketing down on marshland half a metre deep in mud. Gloves not only protect hands from muck and grime inevitably acquired, but more importantly, from that strand of steel cable sticking up, ready to tear through the flesh as the cable is innocently fed through. One tiny strand is enough to cut the palm of a hand. Ideally gloves designed for the job should be worn; these are available from most winching manufacturers, but in extremis leather-palmed gardening gloves are better than nothing.

Always wear leather gloves when handling wire rope

Signalling and communication

Not all winching activities can be accomplished alone; sometimes an assistant can prove invaluable in the operation so it is important that instructions can be communicated clearly to each other. A series of hand-signals has been developed for this purpose and are in general usage.

Hand signals for winching use. At night use a torch in the same way. Use a series of short flashes for taking the strain. Use a whistle blast for emergency stop.

It is important that the signaller should stand in a secure postition where he can see exactly what is happening during the winching operation and be in no immediate danger should things go wrong. He should be able to clearly see the load and be seen by the winch operator. He should face the winch operator if possible and each signal should be distinct and clear. When winching at night, use a torch to convey your instructions in the same way as for hand signals and use a whistle to stop the winching operation in an emergency.

Illustrated are some of the more common signals that are used when winching. LEARN THESE AND USE THEM. If in doubt stop, re-appraise the situation and always proceed with the utmost caution.

Good communications in winching are essential. When signalling, place yourself in a position where you can see the load and the winching operator can see you. A blast of a whistle can be used to stop the winching operation in an emergency.

Twenty-five Steps to Safe Winching

Anyone can become proficient at winching. It is not necessarily an art, but it does require a thorough awareness on the part of the user, as to the capabilities of his winch and equipment coupled with sound knowledge of how to get the best from them. The Winching Technique section covers in some detail the right approach to a winching operation. Listed here is a guide of do's and don'ts of winching operations. Some will be obvious, some not so. All, though, will lead to safer winching.

(1) BEFORE winching with an electric winch, inspect the remote control lead for cracks, pinched wiring, fraying or loose connections. A damaged, shorted lead could cause the winch to operate as soon as it is plugged in.

(2) Only plug in the remote control lead when you want to use the winch.

(3) When the remote control lead is plugged in **ALWAYS** keep it clear of the drum fairlead area, the rope and any rigging.

(4) **ALWAYS** store the control lead in a clean dry area where it cannot be damaged.

(5) When using the remote control from inside the vehicle, **ALWAYS** pass the lead through the window to avoid trapping the lead in the door.

(6) **ALWAYS** stand well clear of wire rope and load during winching operations. Insist that helpers/spectators keep to a safe distance when winching.

(7) **ALWAYS** use vehicle ground anchors when recovering another vehicle.

(8) **ALWAYS** be sure that an anchor point intended for use is strong enough to withstand the load applied.

Adopt a safe operating position. Stand at the side of the vehicle out of the direct line of the pull or operate the winch from inside the vehicle

Vehicle ground anchors provide a secure base for vehicle when using the winch on heavy loads.

(9) **ALWAYS** use a choker chain, wire rope made for the purpose or tree trunk protector when connecting the winch wire to an anchor point.

(10) **ALWAYS** use a tree trunk protector when a tree is used as an anchor point.

(11) **ALWAYS** check that when ground or vehicle anchors are used the anchor is firm throughout the duration of the pull.

(12) **ALWAYS** keep a check on the winch wire anchor point; under heavy load it could fail with disastrous consequences.

(13) **ALWAYS** inspect and carefully re-wind wire rope after use. Crushed, pinched or frayed areas severely reduce original tensile strength. (For safety's sake, wire rope should be replaced when any form of damage is evident).

(14) **ALWAYS** stop winching when the hook is at least 3 metres away from the fairlead of the winch.

Always attach your winch rope to a tree protector. A chain around a tree will certainly hold but may ring-bark the tree. A length of timber inserted on the opposite side to the pull will minimise damage to the bark.

(15) **ALWAYS** wear gloves. Do not let wire rope slide through bare hands.

(16) **ALWAYS** use proper vehicle anchor points. Never hook up to bumpers, spring hangers or axle casings. When recovering an old vehicle be aware of the condition of the vehicle's anchor points.

(17) Ensure that the rope is correctly spooled onto the winch drum. The spooling (winding-on) of the wire rope can be accidentally reversed by running the rope all the way out and re-spooling in with remote control switch in the 'power-out' mode.

(18) **NEVER** handle wire rope or rigging during winching operations or touch a wire rope or its hook while they are under tension; even when the winch is not in operation there may still be a considerable load applied to winch and cable.

Only hook cables to anchor points that are specifically designed for the purpose.

(19) **NEVER** put a wire winch rope round an anchor and hook it back on itself, as this will damage the wire rope and reduce its tensile strength.

(20) **NEVER** operate a winch with less than 5 wraps of wire rope on the drum. A winch drum with fewer than 5 wraps of the rope remaining may break loose under load conditions.

(21) **NEVER** exceed the capacity of the winch. Use a pulley block to double the line-pull which will almost halve the load on the winch and the wire rope.

A minium of 5 coils of wire should always be left on the drum. It would be useful to paint a yellow mark on the cable as the final sixth coil on the drum appears at the fairlead.

A double line-pull can reduce the effort on the winch, and can assist by feeding more cable out to allow the winch to operate closer to its design pull configuration.

A carefully placed log or block of wood will protect the cable and reduce possible wire damage caused by chafing over rocks.

(22) **NEVER** use the winch to tow another vehicle. The braking system on winches is not designed for this sort of abuse and the sudden jerking will eventually cause the wire rope to snap.

(23) **NEVER** stand astride or step over the cable when winching.

(24) **IMPORTANT:** When re-spooling cable, **ALWAYS** release the control switch when the hook is a minimum of 1 metre from the fairlead and inch in the remaining cable onto the drum. This procedure is vital to personal safety and to avoid rope damage caused by over-tightening.

When winching and driving, keep tension on the winch wire. A sudden snatch, as the winch wire alternately becomes slack and takes the load again, will damage the winch and its cable, and will lead to premature cable failure.

(25) When starting winching, use the control switch intermittently to inch in any slack in the wire rope prior to taking the strain. This will reduce the chance of damage to the winch or wire rope from shock loadings (which could briefly exceed the winch's capacity)

Note the use of hand signals: Inching in the winch wire prior to taking the strain.

Ten Steps to Safe Capstan Winch Operation

Operation of the capstan winch poses its own special problems and normally requires two-man operation. Where this is not possible, an emergency engine stop control should be fitted, as close to the front of the vehicle as possible so that in the event of having to stop the winching operation in a hurry, the emergency engine stop-button can be operated.

(1) **ALWAYS** use vehicle ground anchors when winching unless of course conducting self-recovery operations.

(2) It should **ALWAYS** be borne in mind that unlike other winches, the capstan winch cannot be reversed, therefore the load may still be on the rope and when released may allow the load to move. The rope should **ALWAYS** be released with care.

(3) **ALWAYS** keep the free end of the rope clear of the drum.

(4) As with wire ropes, **ALWAYS** check that the rope is of the size and type recommended by the winch manufacturer.

(5) **ALWAYS** check the condition of the rope before use. If it shows signs of wear, discard it and use a new one.

(6) After use **ALWAYS** ensure that the rope is cleaned and dried out (see care of winch ropes).

(7) **NEVER** stand astride the rope when it is under tension. **ALWAYS** control the rope at the side of the vehicle.

(8) **NEVER** wrap the free end of the rope around any part of the body. Should there be any malfunction or breakdown of the winch, serious injury could occur.

Capstan winch in use by H.M. Coastguards for personnel recovery. Good team work is essential for safe winching. Vehicle ground anchors are also essential for this type of work.

(9) **NEVER** stand close to the winch. When conducting vehicle self recovery, always stand well to the side of the vehicle and maintain this stance thoughout the recovery operation.

(10) Should the brass shear pin fail on the capstan winch, replace it only with a genuine replacement part. NB: The shear pin is a safety device designed to fail should the load on the winch exceed the rated capacity.

The Mechanics of Winching

To get the best from a winch and its equipment requires some understanding of the mechanics involved in the winching problem. For winching purposes the resistance to motion of a vehicle is dependent on 4 main factors:-

(i) The inherent resistance to movement of the vehicle.

(ii) The weight of the vehicle.

(iii) The nature of the surface to be transitted.

(iv) The gradient up which the vehicle is to be moved.

(i) The inherent resistance of the vehicle

The inherent resistance to movement of the vehicle depends on the state of its tyres, friction in its drive-chain (which will cause drag), the weight of the vehicle, and whether the vehicle has sustained any damage to its running gear.

For our winching calculations we will assume that the vehicle is in good working order and has its tyres inflated to the recommended pressures - a flat tyre will cause considerable drag, and it may be advisable to change a wheel that has a puncture before commencing recovery operations.

(ii) The weight of the vehicle

The weight of the vehicle is the total weight including all equipment, luggage, fuel, passengers and stores aboard the vehicle.

(iii) The nature of the surface to be transmitted

The nature of the surface to be transitted is the largest variable in the winching equation. A vehicle in good running order on a metalled surface will only require a force of about 1/25 its total weight to induce movement, whereas a vehicle to be recovered from a bog will require a pull equivalent to about 1/2 the total weight of the vehicle. The table below shows that different surfaces require proportionate efforts to produce vehicle movement.

Type of Surface	Effort required to move a vehicle as a fraction of total weight	As a percentage of total weight
Hard metalled road	1/25 total weight of Vehicle	(4%)
Grass	1/7 total weight of Vehicle	(14%)
Sand (hard wet)	1/6 total weight of Vehicle	(17%)
Gravel	1/5 total weight of Vehicle	(20%)
Sand (soft wet)	1/5 total weight of Vehicle	(20%)
Sand (soft/dry/loose)	1/4 total weight of Vehicle	(25%)
Shallow mud	1/3 total weight of Vehicle	(33%)
Bog	1/2 total weight of Vehicle	(50%)
Marsh	1/2 total weight of Vehicle	(50%)
Clay (clinging)	1/2 total weight of Vehicle	(50%)

A simple calculation will show that approximate rolling resistance of an undamaged vehicle on a flat surface can be predicted e.g. the pull required to move a Land Rover Ninety weighing about 2000 kg (4400 lbs) along a flat sandy beach of hard wet sand, co-efficient 1/6.

If we take the weight of the vehicle (in kilogrammes) and multiply it by the co-efficient of the resistance of hard wet sand from the table of efforts required to move a vehicle as a fraction of its total weight, we get the calculation.

Weight of vehicle × co-efficient of wet sand
2000kg × 1/6 = 333kg = effort required to move vehicle in this case

However, as all surfaces are not flat, the calculation must therefore include a gradient resistance co-efficient.

(iv) The gradient up which the vehicle is to be moved

The gradient up which the vehicle is to be moved (gradient resistance) may only cover a short distance over the total distance of the pull, e.g. a ditch or rock, or it may cover a long climb up a hill. Even for a relatively short upward pull, gradient resistance must be taken into account. That the slope to be negotiated to all intents and purposes is only 150mm (6″) high will make no difference to the calculations and should be borne in mind when winching over ridges.

For practical winching purposes, gradient resistance can be taken as 1/60 of the weight of the vehicle for each degree of the slope, up to 45° incline. For inclines over 45° the gradient resistance will be equal to the total weight of the vechicle.

Again a simple calculation can predict the total effort in killogrammes required to move our 2000kgs Land Rover up an incline of 15°

i.e. $\dfrac{\text{Gradient}}{60} \times \text{weight of vehicle}$

which is $\dfrac{15}{60} \times 2000\text{kgs} = 500\text{kgs}$

If we combine the weight of the vehicle, the type of surface to be transitted and the gradient to be overcome we get the calculation.

$$\dfrac{\text{Weight of Vehicle}}{\text{Surface to be transitted}} + \dfrac{(\text{Gradient} \times \text{Weight of Vehicle})}{60}$$

Therefore the winching formula is

$$\dfrac{W}{S} + \dfrac{(G \times W)}{60} = \text{effort required}$$

Where W = Weight of vehicle

S = Surface to be transitted

G = Angle of gradient (in degrees)

Using this winching formula it is now possible to predict the total effort required to move a vehicle in most winching situations.

Example: A Land Rover 90 weighing 2000kgs (4400lbs) is to be winched up a sand dune of dry loose sand with an incline of 15°.

Using the winching formula $\dfrac{W}{S} + \dfrac{(G \times W)}{60}$ = effort required

Where 　　W = 2000kg (vehicle weight)

　　　　　S = 1/4 (co-efficient for dry loose sand)

　　　　　G = 15 (slope in degrees)

We have $\dfrac{2000}{4} + \dfrac{(15 \times 2000)}{60}$ = 500 + 500

= 1000kgs of effort required to recover the vehicle in these circumstances

However, if we substitute clinging clay for the surface (co-efficient of 1/2) and 35 for the gradient (slope) in the above equation we get

$\dfrac{2000}{2} + \dfrac{(35 \times 2000)}{60}$ = 2167 kg (4660 lb) effort required

The effort required in this case may well be beyond the capabilities of the winch because the rating of a winch relates only to the first layer of wire on its drum and available pulling power decreases with each additional layer of wire rope in the winch drum. In the above case, a solution may be to run out all the winch cable to enable the winch to be used at or near its rated capacity, or introduce a pulley into the system to create a mechanical advantage.

The Use of Pulley Blocks in Winching

A very useful winching accessory is the pulley block which, when used in conjunction with the winch, can be rigged to provide a mechanical advantage. There are many types of pulley block, the most common for use with winches employing wire rope being the snatch block. The snatch block is so designed as to permit the bite of a winch cable to be inserted into it.

Fig 1: Shows a snatch block attached at an anchor-point and the cable run from the winch, through the snatch block and hooked back on to the vehicle. This configuration (disregarding certain losses such as friction in the pulley) will give a mechanical advantage to the winch of about 2:1 i.e. the effort required by the winch will be halved. The speed of advance for the vehicle will also be halved for any given winch drum speed, but this can be advantageous in situations where a snatch block is needed. The snatch block also provides a dual advantage for the winch as it reduces the effort required for a given winch drum speed, and, because twice as much wire is required with snatch block configurations, allows a winch to operate with fewer layers on its drum, so it will operate nearer its rated pull configuration (see chart on pages 66 and 67). A snatch block can be useful in many winching situations and can also be used to help create a straight line-pull.

Care must be exercised when using snatch blocks; although they will not necessarily overload the winch, the total weight to be pulled does not change and will still be exerted at the anchor-point.

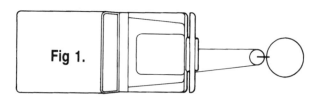

Fig 1.

A pulley block rigged to provide a mechanical advantage of 2:1

A snatch block used to provide a mechanical advantage can be a big help in 'heavy' pull winching operations.

Snatch blocks, used in conjunction with attachment ropes, can be very useful when no convenient anchor point is to hand but recovery direction must be maintained.

Straight Line Pull. Whenever possible, and particularly with drum winches, a straight-line pull is necessary to allow the wire to be evenly spread along the whole surface of the winch drum. If the pull is exerted at an angle, the winch wire may bunch up at one side of the drum which could become wire-bound, the wire bunch may collapse and trap coils under and over each other causing it to bind. Where a straight line-pull is impossible (perhaps where the best anchor-point is not in line with the intended pull direction) a snatch block can be used in conjunction with straps and tree protectors to change the wire feed direction.

This configuration will not provide a mechanical advantage, but will assist when the vehicle must remain on its intended course. Snatch blocks can be used in many winching situations and should not just be restricted to creating the mechanical advantage of a double line-pull.

A snatch block can also be useful for changing the direction of the pull. Although this will not provide any mechanical advantage to the recovery vehicle it does allow greater flexibility of positioning for recovery operations.

Camel Trophy finalists undergo winching instruction by Land Rover's driving team at Eastnor Castle.

Sooner or later, anyone involved in regular winching operations will encounter the problem of having nothing to anchor the winch's cable to, or even secure the vehicle itself when the winch is under load. There can be nothing worse for the wincher than trying to recover a stuck vehicle and dragging himself inexorably into the mire too. In these circumstances some form of anchoring device is obviously required. Winching Anchors fall into two categories:-

(i)   Vehicle Anchors.

(ii) Ground Anchors.

29

Vehicle Anchors

The purpose of vehicle anchors is to prevent the vehicle moving when load is placed on the winch wire. They can be as simple as blocks of wood, rocks or even logs placed in front of the wheels, through to custom-made vehicle anchors specially designed for the job. Vehicle anchors are essential in many winching operations (especially when using a winch to recover a disabled vehicle).

Only those vehicle anchors specifically designed for the purpose offer a high degree of vehicle security and personnel safety, and should be considered as part of the vehicle winching equipment.

Purpose-made vehicle anchors offer a high degree of vehicle security for winch recovery operations.

Ground Anchors

Ground anchors are designed to be inserted into the ground to provide a fixed strong point to which a winch hook may be attached, so that effective self-recovery can be undertaken in the absence of trees or other suitable natural features.

When using the vehicle winch for self-recovery, there will be occasions when there is no convenient or suitable point to which the vehicle winch rope, or wire can be affixed. In this case some suitable anchor for the winch wire will need to be provided. The type of ground anchor will depend largely on the prevailing type of ground: sand, gravel, light-to-heavy soil, mud, clay, bog, or stony ground, all of which require a different approach. Sand and gravel are difficult media in which to secure any anchor, particularly if very loose.

Custom made ground anchors are available which are suitable for a wide variety of ground conditions or ground anchors can be improvised depending on the winching circumstances or prevailing conditions. One method of improvisation of a ground anchor utilises the vehicle spare wheel which when buried sufficiently deep with the largest surface area towards the direction of the pull, will provide an adequate ground anchor and will normally hold fast. The winch cable should be secured through the centre of the spare wheel by a strong bar, such as a half shaft, crow bar or even a thick branch or log.

In fact, the vehicle spare wheel can act as a ground anchor in most situations, but great effort can be required to bury it. Ground anchors can be fashioned from quite simple materials found locally, or items carried which are easily stowable in the vehicle.

The vehicle spare wheel sufficiently buried will provide an adequate ground anchor.

The simple PICKET GROUND ANCHOR can be fashioned from steel stakes driven into the ground. Roped together in this way in light soil or wet ground, this ground anchor should withstand a pull of around 1500kg (3300lbs) for use in boggy conditions, the addition of a spade-type blade fitted to the first stake is advisable and will substantially reduce the tendency of the first stake to pull forward.

The PICKET ground anchor constructed from steel angle iron 25mm x 25mm x 6mm (2" x 2" x ¼") thick by 1.25m (4'6") long. The pickets should be driven into ground for ⅔ this length and firmly roped together. This configuration should withstand a pull of around 1500kg (3300lbs)

In heavier ground or rocky soil or where a sturdier ground anchor is required, the STAKED BAR or PLATE-TYPE ground anchor is ideal. The 'V' plate ground anchor from BUSHEY HALL WINCHES & EQUIPMENT LTD, when correctly deployed in firm ground, should withstand a pull of up to 2000kg. Easily established and recovered, the 'V' plate ground anchor is ideal when a firm anchor point is essential and is also ideal for recovery work.

The custom made MOLEX ground anchor from TIRFOR LTD has been specifically designed for speedy deployment and retrieval. It is suitable for most types of ground conditions and is screwed into the ground with the aid of a pick axe handle or similar tool and depending on ground conditions it should withstand a pull of 1500kg (3300lb). It is ideally suited to casual winching use.

One of the most difficult mediums in which to establish a ground anchor is marshland or large water-logged areas of bog with unstable ground which defies all attempts to establish a firm anchor point. When such conditions are anticipated the DANFORTH anchor may provide the answer. Designed as a small boat's anchor, its tipping flukes can be used to great advantage: when drawn towards the vehicle it will dig into the ground providing a reasonably firm anchor point, suitable for vehicle recovery purposes.

The STAKED BAR ground anchor manufactured by Bushey Hall Winches and Equipment Ltd, is easily established and retrieved, and when used in firm ground can withstand a pull of up to 2 tonne.

The MOLEX ground anchor being deployed.

VEHICLE ANCHOR POINTS

Attaching a winch rope or wire to a vehicle for recovery purposes can prove very difficult. The Land Rover Ninety, One Ten and Range Rover have anchor points fitted to the chassis. Many vehicles do not have designated anchor points, and great care must be exercised here in selecting a suitable point to attach the winch hook; some vehicle damage may be inevitable. On leaf-sprung Land Rovers not fitted with towing and lifting eyes, and for EMERGENCY SITUATIONS ONLY the spring hangers can be used. An inspection of the suspension should be carried out after any such attachment. Under no circumstances should a wire be fastened to the bumper, steering gear or axle casing as these are not designed for this sort of abuse. Many winching manufacturers provide custom made bumpers with their winch fitting kits and these usually have purpose designed built in winching anchor points. It is also possible to fit one of the Land Rover approved lifting and towing attachments to the vehicle. When correctly installed these are ideal for winching use and will be of assistance in vehicle recovery situations.

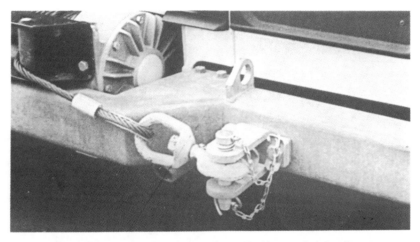

Standard towing jaw Part number 90518674 bolted to the combined bumper winch mounting of the Land Rover Drum winch by Superwinch Ltd.

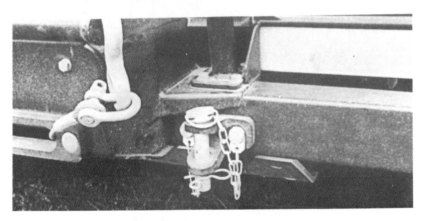

Dixon Bate towing jaw fitted to an expedition-prepared Land Rover One Ten.

Towing ring Part number 559882 fitted with 'D' shackle RTC 7032. The towing ring is secured in place by the bumper fixing bolts.

Towing ring Part number 267950 used here in conjunction with the mounting bracket of the Warn M8274 winch mounting bracket.

It should be borne in mind that both Land Rovers and Range Rovers have provision for winch wire attachments at the rear of the vehicle, the chassis has built in towing eyes and the rear cross member is designed to take a towing attachment. These facilities can also be utilised, not only for winching and vehicle recovery but to provide a hold fast for the vehicle when conducting recovery operations.

A tree protector can double-up as a hold fast, to anchor the vehicle when conducting vehicle recovery operations on soft ground.

NATURAL ANCHOR POINTS

For self-recovery purposes a convenient anchor-point on which to secure the rope or cable is essential. The most commonly used anchor point is a tree. Quite small trees and even saplings can provide an adequate anchor, but take care! A wire or chain round a tree may well ring-bark and kill the tree; always use a tree protector. A shackle should always be used when attaching winch hooks to the tree protectors, straps or ropes. Rocks can also provide a suitable anchor, but chain should be employed rather than a rope or strap to secure the winch hook, as stone tends to cut into these materials. Great care should be exercised when using rocks, as chains can slip off, and the rock although seemingly quite substantial, may not support the load placed on it and may break free from its holding with disastrous results.

When using natural features for an anchor, place the winch wire attachment rope, strap or chain as close to the ground as is practicable to achieve the greatest mechanical advantage from your chosen anchor. Keep a close check on the anchor point whilst weight is placed on it and stop winching at the first signs of the anchor point breaking free.

Where only small bushes or shrubs are available for use as an anchor, the load on a bush can be reduced by roping two together to share the load; however, to give maximum strength these must both be in line with the pull.

Quite small trees and saplings will provide an adequate anchor-point. Place the fastening rope or tree-protector as near to the ground as possible; 2 or 3 turns of rope should be used to spread the load, minimise damage to the tree and prevent the rope slipping.

Good Winching Practice

Take time to assess the winching problem and prepare for your winching operation. Time spent on preparation before you may need to use your winch will minimise rash decisions and careless mistakes.

Rope life is directly related to care and use. On a drum winch the wire rope and any replacement ropes MUST be stretched and wound onto the drum under load. On a new winch this must be carried out before the winch is used. Failure to do so will result in damage to the rope and premature rope failure.

ALWAYS unspool as much rope as possible when preparing for rigging. Double the line-pull with a pulley block, or choose an anchor-point as far away as practical to reduce rope damage, such as crushing and kinking caused by upper layers of cable pulling down into lower layers when short line-pulls are made. The greatest pulling-power available from the winch, which is the winch's designed rated pull, is only available on the first layer of cable on the drum; available pulling power decreases with every additional layer on the winch drum — (see table of Rated Line-Pulls on pages 66 and 67).

ALWAYS pull in as straight a line as possible to reduce build-up of rope at one end of the drum which will reduce the torque available from the winch.

When anchoring the pulling vehicle, apply the brakes and chock wheels. To avoid transmission damage put automatic or manual transmission into neutral.

Heavily used wire. Correctly laid on drum ready for future use.

A Land Rover One Ten prepares for a winching situation. Note the control cable plugged in and control unit passed into the cab. The winch wire has been hooked to the air intake with a short length of light cordage and will be to hand when required.

The winch cable can be held in place to prevent the turns on the drum becoming slack when attaching the winch hook to an anchor point by feeding the cable around a suitable stop, in this case the pintle of the towing hitch, however, the cable must be restored to its normal position before commencing winching. Note the plastic sheeting (fertilizer bag) over the radiator to prevent small leaves and debris clogging the radiator when wading or winching through swamp. It must be removed before normal driving operations commence.

Prepare for your winching operation. When it is anticipated that you will need to use your winch, have the equipment prepared and readily available.

It will sometimes be necessary to respool the winch wire onto the drum without any load on the wire. In these circumstances, to enable the winch wire to be properly relayed onto the drum the correct procedure is to hold the remote control in one hand and winch wire in the other. Stand as far away from the winch as the remote control lead will permit. Operate the switch, 'walk in' a few metres of rope, then stop. Repeat this process until all the winch wire is retrieved.

When retrieving or re-spooling a wire, it is important to distribute winch wire evenly and tightly on the drum to prevent top layers of wire being drawn into bottom layers, creating a 'bind'. If the wire binds on the drum the winch and/or wire may be damaged. A bound winch wire will reel out a short distance and then may be reeled back in, even though the winch remote control is switched in the 'out' position.

Should the wire become bound, run out the cable to the bind, connect the hook to a suitable anchor so that all the slack cable is taken up, then by alternately powering 'in' and 'out' with the winch controller, the wire will usually work itself free. In any event, do NOT put your hands anywhere near the wire when working a 'bind' free.

ALWAYS inspect wire rope after use. Crushed, pinched or frayed areas will severely reduce the original tensile strength. For safety's sake, wire rope should be replaced when any form of damage is evident.

Operate the winch at speed to match the conditions and avoid shock loadings caused through uneven or jerky pulls as these sudden load impulses may exceed the rated strength of the cable and equipment resulting in disastrous premature failures.

No two winching situations are exactly the same and it is impossible to write rules for every eventuality. Experience and common sense will more often than not dictate the right approach to a winching problem. Safety should be the wincher's prime concern.

A purpose designed winching snatch block. Note the correct way of attaching the snatch block to a tree protector/anchor strap.

REMEMBER CARELESS WINCH OPERATION CAN - AND SOMETIMES WILL - RESULT IN DAMAGE TO PROPERTY, SERIOUS INJURY AND EVEN FATALITIES. READ AND UNDERSTAND ALL **SAFETY** PRECAUTIONS AND OPERATING INSTRUCTIONS BEFORE OPERATING A WINCH. THINK "**SAFETY**". ADOPT SAFE WINCHING PRACTICES AND ENJOY YOUR WINCHING.

Care of Wire Ropes

Respect your wire rope and it will respect you

A wire rope is a steel strength member and is designed for specific duties.

The wire rope supplied with Land Rover winch units is designed specifically for pulling operations. It should NEVER be used for lifting without prior consultation with the wire rope manufacturer or equipment supplier who will advise on the stringent and more detailed regulations which then apply.

Make up of a steel wire rope

Wire rope is composed of wires, strands and core. The wires are helically laid together to form a strand. The required number of strands are then helically closed together around the core to form a wire rope.

There are generally two types of core, fibre and steel. Basically each serves the same purpose, to afford support to the strands laid round it.

Wire rope terminations

Swaged or pressed terminations, which are cold pressed or swaged on to the rope, are the type generally fitted by the manufacturer to the Land Rover winch rope. These are designed to take the full breaking load. The neck of the termination and the rope immediately adjacent to it should always be kept in line. This should be borne in mind when using the rope as a choker. An alternative means of attachment, for example a chain, should be wrapped around small objects, such as posts, and a webbing strap or tree protector used on trees.

A cross section of wire rope of the type used on Land Rover winches

This is 6 × 19 (9/9/1) construction with independent wire rope core.

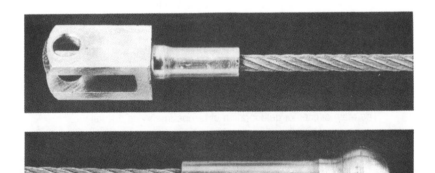

Typical wire rope terminators used on winch cables.

Winch drums

To minimise the loading at the rope anchorage point, a minimum of five dead turns should remain on the drum when the rope is wound out to its maximum operating length.

For maximum rope life, the drum should ideally hold the rope in a single layer, but more often than not this is not possible, because of space restrictions, and several layers are required to accommodate all the rope.

When multi-layering has to be used it should be realized that after the first layer is wound on to a drum, the rope has to cross the underlying rope in order to advance across the drum in the second layer. The points at which the turns in the upper layer cross those in the lower layer are known as the cross-over points and the rope in those areas is susceptible to increased abrasion and crushing.

Care should therefore be taken when operating a winch to ensure that the rope is coiled and layered correctly.

Causes of deterioration

The main causes of deterioration of a rope in service are fatigue, corrosion, abrasion and mechanical damage. One or more of these causes may be present or dominant depending on the duty.

Fatigue in wire ropes is normally caused by repeated bending of ropes under tensile loading, eg when ropes operate over sheaves and around drums.

The main factors affecting fatigue are, therefore, the load on the rope, the ratios of sheaf and drum diameters to rope diameter, rope flexibility and the number of operating cycles.

Ropes are normally lubricated at the manufacturing stage but to increase fatigue life they should be given regular dressings during service.

Corrosion often occurs in combination with fatigue. Except under very dry conditions there is always some corrosion of unprotected (bright) steel wires.

To inhibit the onset of corrosion, ropes should be given frequent applications of suitable dressings during their working life. If there is risk of severe corrosion, it is preferable to use a rope with galvanised wires.

Abrasion occurs primarily in the outer wires. It should be noted that over 50 per cent of the strength of a rope may be in the outer wires.

To prevent the possibility of kinking or disturbance of the lay, ropes should be paid out without slack and in a straight line. Kinks that occur in handling or in service that leave a permanent bend in the rope can reduce its strength by up to 50 per cent.

Examination and maintenance.

The continued safe operation of appliances and systems employing wire ropes depends to a large extent on the regular assessment of the condition of the ropes and the equipment with which they are used.

Good maintenance will, in general, increase the ropelife. This is especially so where corrosion and fatigue are the main causes of deterioration. In these cases, regular cleaning and service dressing is a necessary part of good maintenance.

Wherever possible, inspections should be carried out at the beginning of each work period, and, when experience so indicates, at intermediate periods.

An inspection should also be carried out immediately following any incident which could have damaged the rope or the installation.

When carrying out inspections and examinations to assess the fitness of the rope for further service, it is necessary to consider both general deterioration and localised deterioration or damage. Particular attention should be paid to the rope adjacent to the terminations, lengths that have been running or stationary over the drum and any other areas likely to sustain damage.

The maintenance of general purpose wire ropes is normally confined to cleaning, application of dressings and the removal of occasional broken wire ends. It is essential to note the condition of the rope in the vicinity of a wire break, because more than one break within a short distance could indicate the onset of more serious problems.

The point of attachment is particularly prone to deterioration.

A rope may continue in operation with broken wires, but an early opportunity should be taken to remove the protruding ends. Nipping off the broken wires with pliers is not the best method for this leaves a jagged end. A better method is to use a pair of pliers to bend the wire backwards and forwards until it breaks inside the rope.

If a wire rope has broken wires generally distributed along its length it should be discarded.

Wire rope dressings and lubrication

The importance of lubrication has already been stressed. Good general purpose lubricating oils are normally suitable.

Wherever practical a dressing should be applied as soon as the rope is first put to work. It should be re-applied at regular intervals and before the rope is showing signs of corrosion or dryness.

There are several methods of applying dressings and the most suitable for any particular rope depends upon the viscosity of the dressing and the length of rope involved. The methods of application include brushing, spraying, dripfeed, running through a bath or by automatic applicators.

For maximum effect, the lubricant should be applied if possible to the rope where it 'opens up' as it travels over the drum.

If the existing dressing on the rope is heavily loaded with dirt, sand grit, etc. or if loose corrosion products are present, these should be removed with a wire brush or other suitable means.

Always use protective gloves when handling wire ropes and remember, always stand well clear when a wire rope is under load to avoid whiplash of the free ends in the event of breakage or the rope pulling free.

Engineering wire ropes in accordance with British standards

Land Rover Parts Number	Diameter Size	Construction	Minimum Breaking load (tonnes)
RTC 7028	8 mm	6 × 19 with steel core	4.11
RTC 7029	9 mm	6 × 19 with steel core	5.22
RTC 7040	10 mm	6 × 19 with steel core	6.44

NB These breaking loads are based on static tensile testing. Mechanical damage, eg. kinking, wear, etc. can reduce the above breaking loads dramatically.

Care should be taken when selecting replacement wire ropes for drum winches. Only wire rope specifically designed for its intended usage should be used. Further information on selecting the correct replacement wire rope for your specific winch can be obtained from the winch supplier or from a specialist winch wire/rope manufacturer. Ropes manufactured by British Ropes Ltd meet all required specifications. For further information contact the equipment supplier or the rope manufacturer.

BRITISH ROPES LIMITED

Carr Hill

Doncaster

South Yorkshire DN4 8DG

Telephone: (0302) 344010

Telex 547981

The following guidance is intended for users of fibre ropes operating in pulling applications.

If ropes are to be used for lifting, more stringent and detailed safety regulations apply. Do not, therefore, use a rope for lifting without first consulting the rope manufacturer, equipment supplier or other qualified and competent person.

In the choice of rope for any application, guidance should be sought from the rope maker or supplier, BRIDON FIBRES LIMITED, Dunston, Gateshead, Tyne & Wear NE8 2QY: Tel: 091 4605061; Telex: 53459.

Uncoiling Cordage

Lengths of cordage are usually supplied in a coil which may have a label tied at one end saying 'This side up. Take from this end.' Provided that this simple instruction is followed, the rope should run from the coil without difficulty. Should the label have become detached, it is possible to start removing the rope from the coil the wrong way. Kinks will occur in the rope and these should not be tolerated since they may contribute to serious damage of the rope in subsequent use. Replace the length of rope which has been withdrawn into the centre of the coil. Turn the coil over. Reach into the centre and draw the end upwards. The rope should then run correctly from the coil without kinking.

An improvement of this practice of pulling the rope from the centre of the coil is to lay the coil flat on a cross of wood having a ringbolt at its centre. The cross bearing the coil is suspended by the ring and the rope taken from the outside of the coil by rotating the whole assembly. This is the best way to attempt this task but is cumbersome and impracticable in many instances. Alternatively, the coil of rope may be placed on a turntable which is rotated to take the rope from the coil.

Coiling Cordage

Always coil right hand laid rope in a clockwise direction and left hand laid rope in an anti-clockwise direction. Use as large a circle as is practical when coiling down. When the rope has been coiled, hang it up in a dry atmosphere away from fires, steam pipes etc. to prevent its being damaged. Plaited ropes may be coiled in either direction or may be flaked in a 'figure of eight' formation.

Pulleys and Sheaves

If the rope is to be used in conjunction with a pulley, ensure that the pulley size is adequate for the rope. Man-made fibre ropes will run over very small rope/pulley diameter ratios. Normally, the pulley should not be smaller than five rope diameters. Should it be necessary to reduce this ratio further, the manufacturer's advice should be sought. It is stressed that the pulley diameter should be as large as is practical for the application. A penalty of higher wear and lower rope life is the result of reducing the pulley size.

The profile of the pulley grooving is also important. The groove should support the rope over approximately one third of its circumference. Too tight or too flat a groove will increase the incidence of rope wear by increasing the deformation of the rope where it passes around the pulley.

Finally, ensure that the pulley receives adequate maintenance so that it does, in fact, rotate with the rope. It is surprising how many hand tackles are seen with pulleys which have seized owing to an absence of lubrication and a build-up of fibre dust on the pulley spindles. The ropes slide over static pulleys producing a high polish on the bearing surfaces, reducing the mechanical advantage and shortening the rope life. A minimal amount of maintenance would overcome this problem.

Use and Care Recommendations

Rope of whatever material is liable to wear-and-tear. It can suffer mechanical damage or be weakened by chemicals, heat, light etc. Safe rope usage depends on the quality of materials and workmanship; fibre ropes must conform to British Standards. Man-made fibre ropes are less prone to gradual weakening through use than natural fibre ropes, but as well as statutory thorough examinations by a competent person (Health & Safety at Work Act) all types of fibre rope must be regularly and frequently inspected to ensure their serviceability. No matter what has caused the weakening of a fibre rope, the effect will be more serious on smaller sizes. Rope should be used that has an adequate cross-section for the given application taking into account the rigours of mechanical damage.

Examination of sections measuring about 300mm (1ft) at a time is recommended, turning the rope to reveal all surfaces and twisting the strands slightly to inspect between them. With natural fibre ropes, firm 'wringing' at intervals may reveal a form of fibre powder (a de-naturing or embrittlement of the fibre) but this test must be done carefully to avoid upsetting the rope-lay. Defining an acceptable standard is harder than deciding the test method. There is no clear division between safe and unsafe ropes as it depends on the stresses placed upon a rope in an emergency. The decision to use or discard a rope must be based on assessment of its overall condition since many of the conditions cannot be described in exact terms, and sound judgement on this will only come through experience. It is always better to err on the side of caution and discard rope whose quality is doubtful. Ropes can be replaced, lives cannot. It is important to understand that mechanical damage is far worse on smaller ropes than on larger sizes, as most of their yarns are on the outside of the strand, which makes them vulnerable to severing over short distances, e.g. heavy chafing which has a dramatic effect on the rope strength. Larger ropes have strands composed of concentric rings of yarns, so chafing has to be correspondingly deeper to achieve the same effect.

Causes of Damage

- The most obvious cause of weakness is external wear, due to dragging over rough surfaces, causing breakdown of filaments and fibres. In the extreme, strands become so worn that their outer faces are flattened and outer yarns severed. In ordinary use some disarrangement or breakage of the fibres is unavoidable, and to a certain extent harmless.

- Local abrasion may be caused by rope passing over a sharp edge while under tension causing serious loss of strength. Slight damage to outer fibres, and an occasional torn yarn are harmless, but serious reduction in the area of one strand warrants rejection. Protection of the rope at points where excessive abrasion may occur is a safety and economic measure.

- Cuts, contusions, careless use etc. can cause internal damage which may be indicated by local rupturing or loosening of the yarns or strands.

- Internal wear caused by repeated loading and flexing of the rope, can be accelerated by penetration of grit or other sharp particles into the cross-section of rope, indicated by very loose strands or by powdered fibre dust within the rope.

- Rope should NEVER BE OVERLOADED. Load-bearing ropes should only be used to take their safe working load as marked. Repeated overloading results in permanent elongation of the rope, considerably reducing the energy absorption capability in an emergency.

- Mildew does not attack man-made fibre ropes, though contamination under certain circumstances can provide a nutrient that permits growth of moulds. Unpleasant, but not weakening to the rope, and removable by washing in water. Use of harsh detergents should be avoided. Mildew attacks natural fibre ropes if stored wet in stagnant air. The mould lives on the cellulose of the rope and loss in strength inevitably occurs.

- When stored, ropes should be protected from damp, heat and the effects of sunlight (direct/ through glass). It is advantageous to hang them on wooden pegs or galvanised hooks in a well-ventilated store, air freely circulating at a temperature of 10-20C (50-70F), relative humidity of 40-60%. Even in well-ventilated stores certain air pockets can become stagnant and these should not be used for rope storage. A shed in the yard is a suitable place, ventilated, preferably with wooden roof or material other than corrugated iron. The above is ideal for all fibre ropes but particularly for natural fibre.

- When wet or damp, natural fibre ropes should not be left on the ground as this is how germs of rot start, and grit particles are picked up. Man-made fibre ropes, though not affected by damp, are liable to grit damage. Wet ropes should be hung over pegs in freely circulating air and allowed to dry naturally. If this is impossible, they should be loosely stacked, clear of damp ground or sweating concrete. Coils of new rope should also be stacked thus. ROPES SHOULD NEVER BE DRIED BY ARTIFICIAL HEAT.

- Chemical attack meets little resistance in natural fibre ropes, the only safeguard being to avoid all contact with chemicals; if contamination is suspected, rope should be discarded for lifting purposes. Man-made fibre ropes have high resistance to chemical attack, varying according to type, e.g. Polyamide (nylon) has outstanding resistance to fairly high concentrations of alkalis, but is attacked by acids, while Polyester fibre ropes resist high concentrations of acid, but are attacked by strong alkalis. Polypropylene fibre ropes, though not as strong as Polyamide or Polyester of equal size, are virtually immune from acid or alkaline attack, but not from industrial solvents. If contamination is suspected of:

a) Polyamide (nylon) rope with acid,

b) Polyester rope with alkalis,

c) Polypropylene with organic solvent,

the rope should IMMEDIATELY BE WITHDRAWN FROM SERVICE. A number of rust-removing compounds incorporate acidic active ingredients which degrade Polyamide (nylon), and natural fibres. If contamination of a rope is unavoidable reference should be made to the rope manufacturer regarding the choice of an appropriate material.

- Extreme heat can cause charring of natural fibres and fusing of man-made fibres. Any sign of heat damage warrants rejection of the rope, but it can be severely weakened by heat without it being visible. Again, the best safeguard is proper care in use and storage. Avoid contact with hot surfaces, and keep it clear of hot gases, e.g. blow lamps or welding torches.

- Fibre ropes are subject to degradation by sunlight, like any other textile product, but tests have shown that man-made fibre cordage produced to British Standards, that require certain additives, will degrade less rapidly than natural fibre ropes, whose performance in this respect has stood the test of time.

- When exposed to sulphur dioxide fumes, natural fibre ropes have been known to be severely attacked particularly if wet. Ropes exposed to noxious fumes should be very carefully stored. Frequent and thorough inspections should be carried out by a competent person.

Man-made fibre ropes are easy to handle when wet or dry, they have low water absorption properties and are immune to rot from mildew or marine decay. Each of the types of man-made fibre ropes has its own peculiarities and characteristics which determine its use for particular service. The man-made fibre rope recommended for use with capstan winches fitted to Land Rovers and Range Rovers is 24mm Polypropylene rope layered as a three-strand hawser.

Breaking strains of man-made fibre ropes.

The table below lists the minimum breaking load expected for the three main types of man-made fibre rope available.

Diameter (mm)	Minimum Breaking Load tonnes		
	Nylon	Polyester	Polypropylene
22mm	10.00	7.62	6.50
24mm	12.00	9.14	7.60
26mm	13.90	10.70	8.80

Nylon (BS3977:1966) The strongest man-made fibre has exceptional resistance to sustained loading, has a high energy-absorbing capacity and resists oils, organic solvents and alkalis.

Polyester (BS3758:1964) Retains its strength when either wet or dry, resists acids and is unaffected by oil, organic solvents and bleaching agents.

Polypropylene (BS4928:1973) A lightweight man-made fibre rope which is highly resistant to oils, acids and alkalis. However, it can be affected by bleaching agents and some industrial solvents.

Land Rover Approved Winches

Land Rover Limited approve certain winches for fitment to Land Rovers. A table covering Land Rover approved drum winches for electrical, mechanical and hydraulic drive is shown here. These winches can be fitted at manufacture by Land Rover Limited — contact your Land Rover dealer for further details. All of the approved winches covered in this section are available for retrospective fit, some have been selected for supply through your local Land Rover Parts Agent, and relevant part numbers for these winches are included in the specifications

It is stressed that when these approved winches are fitted for use on a Land Rover, single line pulls in excess of 2268kg (5000lbs) should not be attempted — see Mechanics of Winching section for winching formulae for approximate winch loading calculations. For a winch operation involving a pull of more than 2268kg (5000lbs) it is strongly emphasised that a snatch block must be used.

It is equally important that the winch should always be operated within the certified breaking strain of the wire rope being used.

LAND ROVER APPROVED DRUM WINCHES — ELECTRICAL

MANUFACTURER TECHNICAL DATA SUPPLIER			RYDERS INTERNATIONAL KNOWSLEY ROAD BOOTLE LIVERPOOL L20 4NW		WARN INTERNATIONAL, SEATTLE, U.S.A.				SUPERWINCH LTD ABBEY RISE WHITCHURCH ROAD TAVISTOCK DEVON PL18 9DR	
Manufacturer Identification L.R. Part Number			Warn M8000 Low Profile RTC 8881		Warn M8274 Upright RTC 8013		Warn M10000 Low Profile —		HUSKY RTC 8137	
RATED LINE PULL	Figures as kgs(lbs) quoted in manfacturers literature		kg 3630	(lbs) (8000)	kg 3630	(lbs) (8000)	kg 4536	(lbs) (10000)	kg 3855	(lbs) (8500)
Approved line pull for use with Land-Rovers Single line pull kg (lbs)		1st Lay	2040	(4500)	2040	(4500)	2268	(5000)	2040	(4500)
		2nd Lay	2040	(4500)	2040	(4500)	2268	(5000)	2040	(4500)
		3rd Lay	2040	(4500)	2040	(4500)	2268	(5000)	2040	(4500)
		4th Lay	2040	(4500)	2040	(4500)	2268	(5000)	2040	(4500)
		5th Lay	—	—	—	—	2268	(5000)	2040	(4500)
		6th Lay	—	—	—	—	—	—	1860	(4100)
LINE SPEED First lay line-pull performance at various loads with corresponding approximate motor currents	kg	(lbs)	mtr/min	amperes	mtr/min	amperes	mtr/min	amperes	mtr/min	amperes
	0	(0)	7	97	13.5	62	9.75	62	6	65
	250	(550)	5.5	120	10.5	110	8.0	90	5.5	85
	500	(1100)	4.8	150	8.25	140	7.0	115	4.5	100
	1000	(2200)	3.9	200	4.0	225	4.5	180	3.0	140
	1500	(3300)	2.9	265	2.9	300	3.0	250	2.5	170
	2000	(4400)	2.5	320	2.00	380	2.0	280	2.0	200
	2250	(5000)	2	360	1.5	410	1.5	330	1.5	210
OVERLOAD PROTECTION			None		None		Thermal Cut-Out		None	
CONTROL SYSTEM			Solenoid pack with 3.7m remote control 'Wander' lead providing powering 'in' or 'out' facility						Remote control with 3 metres wander lead	
GEAR TRAIN/RATIO			216.1		3 Stage planetary Spur Gears 134.1		164.1		Worm 8 wheel 294.1	
BRAKING			Automatic		Automatic		Automatic		Automatic	
FREE SPOOLING			Yes		Yes		Yes		Yes	
RECOMMENDED CABLE SIZE	Ordinary Lay W.B.C Rope Dia mm Rope length mtr (ft)		6 x 36 8 24 (80)		6 x 36 8 36 (117)		7 x 19 10 38 (125)		6 x 19 8 46 (150)	
WEIGHT			kg (lbs)		kg (lbs)		kg (lbs)		kg (lbs)	
	Winch		27 (60)		38 (84)		41 (90)		31 (68)	
	Cable		7 (15)		10 (22)		14 (31)		13 (28)	
	Mounting kit		10 (22)		16 (36)		15 (33)		25 (55)	
MODEL APPLICABILITY	Land-Rover Range-Rover		Yes Yes		Not with air con Not auto or air con		Yes Yes		Yes (RTC 8737) Yes (RTC 8138)	
RECOMMENDED EXTRAS Factory fitment			EXTRA HEAVY DUTY BATTERY (17 PLATE) 90 amp Variant VD03N Part No. PRC1501							
			NOTE: Electric winches are intended primarily for intermittent operation. Lengthy periods of continuous operation will cause overheating of the winch motor							
OPTIONAL EXTRAS	Split charge system		Alternative cable 9mm x 68 (21) Snatch Block Galvanised hook 24 volt option available Roller fairlead		Alternative cable 9mm x 100(30) Snatch block Galvanised hook 24 volt option available		Snatch block Galvanised hook 24 volt option available		Roller fairlead Snatch block cable 24 volt option available	

LAND ROVER APPROVED DRUM WINCHES
MECHANICAL AND HYDRAULIC

		MECHANICAL		HYDRAULIC	
MANUFACTURER TECHNICAL DATA		Superwinch Ltd Abbey Rise Whitchurch Road Tavistock Devon PL19 9DR	Superwinch Ltd Abbey Rise Whitchurch Road Tavistock Devon PL19 9DR	Ryders International Knowsley Road Bootle Liverpool L20 4NW	Bushey Hall Winches & Equipment Ltd Unit 7 Lismirrane Ind. Park, Elstree Rd, Elstree Hertfordshire WD6 3EE
Manufacturers Identification & Part Number		8000 Drum RTC8888	10000 Drum —	Warn M10000HY —	Ramsey IPH 8000 —
RATED LINE-PULL Single Line-Pull	Figures as quoted in manufacturers literature	kg (lbs) 3630 (8000)	kg (lbs) 4536 (10000)	kg (lbs) 4536 (10000)	kg (lbs) 3630 (8000)
Approved Line-Pull for use with Land Rovers Single Line Pull (lbs)	1st Lay	2268 (5000)	2268 (5000)	2268 (5000)	2268 (5000)
	2nd Lay	2268 (5000)	2268 (5000)	2268 (5000)	2268 (5000)
	3rd Lay	2268 (5000)	2268 (5000)	2268 (5000)	2268 (5000)
	4th Lay	2268 (5000)	2268 (5000)	2268 (5000)	2213 (4680)
	5th Lay	2268 (5000)	2268 (5000)	2268 (5000)	1968 (4340)
LINE SPEED at lay performance various loads with corresponding motor currents	AT 1000 RPM engine speed based upon Average Drum Diameter	mtr/min (ft/min)	mtr/min (ft/min)		mtr/min (ft/min)
	1st gear	2.72 (9)	2.72 (9)		1.5 (5.0)
	2nd gear	4.24 (14)	4.24 (14)	No data available	2.6 (8.5)
	3rd gear	6.46 (21)	6.46 (21)		6.4 (21)
	4th gear	9.75 (32)	9.75 (32)		9.7 (32)
	5th gear	11.73 (38)	11.73 (38)		—
	Reverse	2.63 (8)	2.63 (8)		—
OVERLOAD PROTECTION		Adjustable Load limiter	Relief Valve	Relief valve	Relief valve
CONTROL SYSTEM		Engagement lever on winch P.t-o. engagement in cab of vehicle			
GEAR TRAIN/RATIO		Worm 8 wheel 48.1	Worm 8 wheel 48.1	3 Stage planetary spur gears 27.1	120.1
BRAKING		Automatic	Automatic	Automatic	Automatic
LINE SPOOLING		Yes	Yes	Yes	Yes
RECOMMENDED CABLE SIZE	Ordinary Lay, W.B.C. Rope Dia (mm) Rope Length mtr (ft)	6 x 19 9 77 (250)	6 x 19 9 77 (250)	6 x 19 10 30 (100)	7 x 19 10 30 (100)
WEIGHT	Winch kg (lbs) Cable Mounting Kit	48 (106) 22 (48) 44 (97)	48 (106) 22 (48) 44 (97)	36 (80) 22 (48) 15 (33)	45 (100) 15 (33) 60 (132)
MODEL APPLICABILITY	Land Rover Range Rover	Yes No	Yes No	Yes No	Yes No
RECOMMENDED EXTRA	Factory Fitment	Hand throttle	Hand Throttle	Hand Throttle	Hand Throttle
OPTIONAL EXTRAS		Alternative Cable 11mm x 46mtr Ground Anchor Pay on lever	Alternative Cable 11mm x 46mtr Ground Anchor Pay on lever	Alternative Cable 11mm x 46mtr	Alternative Cable 8mm x 30mtr 9mm x 26mtr
NOTE					Additional weight of hydraulic power pack 66kg (145lbs)

The Land Rover Drum Winch

Superwinch Ltd, formerly F.W. Winches Ltd., (Fairey Winches) and originally Mayflower Automotive Products, are well respected as suppliers of winches for Land Rovers and Range Rovers and their mechanical drum winch is a heavy duty unit designed for adverse working environments.

The drum winch, driven from the centre power take-off position has become the first choice of fleet users who require a high capacity unit with low maintenance requirements. An interesting development of this unit is an automatic overload protection clutch, instead of the more traditional brass shear-pin type of overload device. Briefly the clutch forms part of the power take-off drive unit mounted on the back of the transfer box. This fail-safe system should be pre-set at installation to take a maximum first layer line-pull of 2268kg (5,000lb) thereby ensuring that a winch overload situation will not arise. The unit has a free spooling clutch and is fully reversible under load conditions. The unit has a built-in roller guide and the kit comes complete with all drive components.

Specification

SWL max: Bare drum 3630kg (8000lbs) (This should be pre-set on installation to 2268kg (5000lbs)

P.t-o Ratio 1:1

Worm box ratio 48:1 (fully self-sustaining fail-safe under load)

Maximum rope length 46m (11mm rope), 77m (9mm rope)

Line speeds; (Based on average drum diameter) with engine speed at 1000 RPM:- First Gear 2.72mtr/min

Second Gear 4.24mtr/min

Third Gear 6.46mtr/min

Fourth Gear 9.75mtr/min

Fifth Gear 11.73mtr/min

Reverse Gear 2.63mtr/min

Total weight of unit including winch, bumper, shafting and P.t-o — 93kg

Weight of rope — 9mm, 32.3kg per 100mtr

11m, 48.2kg per 100mtr

Superwinch Ltd, Abbey Rise, Whitechurch Road, Tavistock, Devon PL19 9DR; Tel: (0822) 614101/7; FAX (0822) 615204

Available world wide through Land Rover Parts Limited Agents

Part number   RTC 8888 — Drum Winch complete with wire rope.

The most recent winch development from SUPERWINCH LIMITED is their first electric winch, the Husky. The Husky is a 3850kg (8500lb) line-pull unit suitable for both private and commercial use. The Husky's combined bumper and fixing kit forms a very neat and compact unit. The winch control box is designed to be sited behind the front grille, well out of harm's way. The rugged construction of the Husky, being of heat treated aluminum and steel, combines light weight with strength. The drive for the winch drum is through a phosphor bronze worm wheel and a 65 tonne nickel chrome high tensile steel case hardened worm, both mounted in substantial roller bearings, ensuring a high degree of safety in operation. The worm drive is self locking assuring absolute safety. A totally enclosed multi-spline clutch operated by an easy action lever disengages the drum to allow free spooling of the wire rope. The Husky is everything you would expect from a company that is world famous for its Land Rover winches.

Specification

Husky Rated Line Pull: 3850kg (8500lbs)

Gear Reduction Ratio: 294:1

Rope Type: 6 x 19 (9/9/1) Steel Core Galvanised Wire Rope,

Min Breaking Load 4110kg (9,060lbs)

Drum Capacity: 8mm rope x 46mtr (5/16ins × 150ft)

Motor Power: 12 volts — 1.4kw (1.9hp); 24 volt — 1.6kw (2.1hp)

Weight: 31kg (68lb)

Load kg (lb)	Rope Speed		12v Motor	24v Motor
	mtr/min	(ft/min)	(amperes)	(amperes)
0	6.2	(20.5)	65	40
900 (2000)	3.1	(10.2)	125	70
1800 (4000)	2.1	(7.0)	190	105
2700 (6000)	1.5	(5.0)	255	140
3600 (8000)	1.1	(3.5)	320	170

Available worldwide through Land Rover Parts Limited Agents:-

Part Number

Husky Electric Winch complete with fitting kit, wire rope, hook and remote control unit.

RTC 8137   Land Rover Ninety/One Ten

RTC 8138   Range Rover

The Land Rover Capstan winch by SUPERWINCH LIMITED is a very popular fitment. The winch is easy to install (approx 2½hr), easy to operate and very versatile and is ideally suited for self-recovery and general winch work. The latest unit designed for the Land Rover Ninety and One Ten has a substantial bull bar incorporated in its mounting kit. This winch is available in either short bollard (illustrated) or tall bollard. Driven directly from the crankshaft with a single line-pull of 1815kg (4,000lbs), the unit is available to fit Land Rover Series II, IIA, III, Ninety, One Ten on 4 cylinder engine models, and Land Rover Series III, Ninety, One Ten on V8 models. Overload protection is by a brass shear-pin type fail-safe system. The drive-shaft has been designed to allow quick disconnection for fan belt changes.

Specification

SWL.	1820kg (4000lbs)
Worm Box ratio:	6:1
Recommended rope:	Terylene/Polyester
Size diameter:	20mm
Rope length:	as required
Line Speed: at 1000rpm engine speed:	8.7mtr/min

Fully self-sustaining fail-safe under load, overload protection by shear-pin (use shear-pin 5095-A4)

Optional extras	Rope

Available worldwide through Land Rover Parts Limited Agents

Part number

RTC 8874   Land Rover Ninety/One Ten four cylinder models

Manufactured in America by Warn Industries, the Warn M8274 upright model winch has a 3600kg (8000lbs) single line-pull capability and its large drum can accommodate up to 45mtr of 8mm wire rope. The M8274's drive train spur gears run in their own oil bath to give longer life under heavy usage. The winch has an automatic brake in both power-in and power-out modes and an easy action pull/push type free-spooling clutch, which can be easily operated even when wearing winching gloves. The M8274 can be fitted to all Land Rovers with the exception of those fitted with air conditioning. The M8274 with its easy-to-fit winch mounting bracket and winch mounted control box make this winch a popular fitment to Land Rovers.

Specification

Rated Line Pull 3600kg (8000lbs)

Wire Rope Diameter 8mm

Drum Capacity up to 45mtr × 8mm rope

Horse Power (12 volt unit) 2.1

Gear Ratio 134:1

M8274 First Layer Performance at Various Loads

Load (kg)	Line Speed (m.per minute)	AMP. Draw (12 Volts)
0	13.6	62
1000	4.4	241
1500	3.1	318
2000	1.9	394
2500	1.4	450
3000	0.9	522
3600	0.4	585

U.K. Distributor for Warn Winches:- Ryders International,

Knowsley Road, Bootle, Liverpool L20 4NW

Available worldwide from Land Rover Parts Limited Agents

Part number

RTC 8013	M8274 "UPRIGHT MODEL" Winch
RTC 8105	Fitting Kit Ninety/One Ten except air-con. models
RTC 8015	Fitting Kit Range Rover (pre 1986 MY) without automatic transmission or air-conditioning
RTC 8014	Fitting Kit Series III (except V8)

The Warn M8000 low-profile winch is suitable for fitting to most Land Rover and Range Rover models, including those fitted with air conditioning. This winch fitment provides a particularly neat installation and its insignficant appearance belies its capability to give a direct line-pull of 3600kg (8000lbs). The compactness of this unit is due to the three-stage planetary gearing employed in the drive chain. Special safety features are the automatic brake which operates on both power-in and power-out modes, and incorporated into the design is an easily operated free-spooling clutch. This sturdy winch fitment is well suited to vehicle recovery and general winching.

Specification

M8000 Rated Line Pull 3600kg (8000lbs)

Wire Rope Diameter 8mm

Wire Rope Length 24mtr

Horse Power (12 volt unit) 1.8

Gear Ratio 216:1

M8000 First Layer Performance of Various Loads

Load (kg)	Line Speed (mtr/minute)	Current Draw (12 volts)
0	6.6	97
1000	4.2	219
1500	3.1	280
2000	2.6	338
2500	2.1	395
3000	1.6	449
3600	1.1	501

Available worldwide from Land Rover Parts Limited Agents

Part number

RTC 8881   M8000 Low Profile Winch

RTC 8882   Fitting Kit Land Rover Ninety/One Ten

RTC 8883   Fitting Kit Range Rover

The Ramsey IPH 8000 Hydraulic Winch

The Ramsey IPH 8000 hydraulic planetary gear drum winch from BUSHEY HALL WINCHES AND EQUIPMENT LTD is a powerful 3630kg (8000lbs) line pull machine which incorporates the very latest in planetary gear drives which produces very little heat allowing the winch to run almost continuously. The IPH 8000 Hydraulic Winch kit includes a hydraulic oil reservoir complete with filters and sight gauge, replacement bumper and all controls. Valve control of this winch is by Electric Solenoid enabling the winch to be operated by both hand held remote control and with a normal hand control valve which is sited on the bumper adjacent to the winch. On manual control valve operation, the winch gives very precise speed control taking it from 10mtr per min to fine 'feathering' adjustments.

Specification

IPH 8000 Hydraulic Rated Line Pull   3630kg (8000lbs)

Rope diameter 8mm or 9mm

Drive System   Closed Loop Hydraulic

Gearing   3 stage plantetary: 120:1 — running in oil

Braking System   (1) Motor Brake — Provides Dynamic Braking

(2) Spring Applied Friction Brake — Holds the load

with no slippage when the winch is stopped

Free Spool   The Clutch Handle has a Spring Loaded Catch which gives

Positive Locking

Clutch Engagement is by Multi-spline coupling activated every 9° of

Drum Rotation

Construction   Aluminium with steel drum

Maximum Line Pull per Layer	9mm Rope	10mm Rope
First Layer	3630kg (8000lbs)	3630kg (8000lbs)
Second Layer	3029kg (6679lbs)	2956kg (6518lbs)
Third Layer	2621kg (5780lbs)	2330kg (5138lbs)
Fourth Layer	2312kg (5098lbs)	2213kg (4880lbs)
Fifth Layer	2067kg (4557lbs)	1968kg (4340lbs)

Available from:-

Bushey Hall Winches and Equipment Ltd,

Unit 7, Lismirrane Industrial Park,

Elstree Road, Elstree, Borehamwood,

Hertfordshire WD6 3EE

Tel: 01-953 6050 Fax: 01-207 5308

The TU16H model is basically a standard Tirfor TU16 hand winch which has been modified by fitting a reciprocating hydraulic ram to remove the manual effort, although the winch can still be hand-operated in emergencies. The unit is normally stowed in the rear of the vehicle and is only fitted when required for use, when it may be anchored to either the vehicle itself or to some other convenient anchorage point. It is then powered by a hydraulic pack fitted to the vehicle, via self-sealing couplings, and operated by a control valve located inside the driving compartment. The winch is a reversible unit and also has a free-spooling facility for rapid pay out of the winch cable.

A "Coilmatic" automatic cable coiling device is available for fitting to the winch which will prevent the free cable getting tangled with the

80

vehicle when self-recovering; it will also help prevent damage to the cable and so increase its working life.

Specification

Tirfor TU16H Rated Line Pull   2270kg (5000lbs)

Nominal working capacity   1600kg (3500lbs)

Wire Rope diameter   11.3mm (0.44ins)

Wire Rope Length with coilmatic drum   20mtr (65ft)

Wire Rope Length without coilmatic drum   UNLIMITED

Weight of Unit (complete)   28kg (62lbs)

Weight of standard 20 metres (65ft) wire-rope (with reeler) 13kg (29lbs)

Wire Rope movement per complete to and fro stroke of cylinder ram:

Forward with load of 1600kg (3500lbs) approx 37mm (1.46ins)

Reverse with load of 1600kg (3500lbs) approx 44mm (1.74ins)

Minimum breaking load of wire-rope 8128kg (17920lbs)

When pressure gauge reads:	Load on wire-rope is approximately:
45 bars (660 psi)	363kg (800lb)
65 bars (955 psi)	800kg (1760lb)
90 bars (1325 psi)	1200kg (2600lb)
115 bars (1690 psi)	1600kg (3500lb)
140 bars (2060 psi)	2000kg (4440lb)

Available from:

Tirfor Limited, Holbrock Industrial Estate,

Old Lane, Halfway, Sheffield, South Yorkshire S19 5GZ

Tel: (0743) 482266, Telex 54354 TIRFOR G

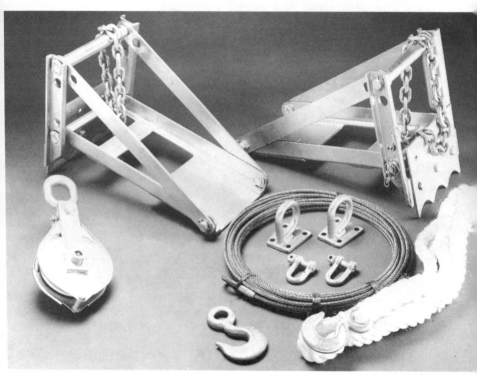

To exploit the full potential of your winch, Land Rover Parts Limited have developed a comprehensive range of winching accessories which include vehicle anchors, pulley blocks, towing and lifting eyes, cordage and wire rope, hooks and shackles. All accessories in this range have been chosen for their reliability and suitability for use with Land Rovers and Range Rovers. All stress items are individually certified. The full range of accessories are available worldwide through Land Rover Parts Limited Agents.

ROPE HOOKS AND D-SHACKLES

The purpose designed rope hook Part number RTC 7031

and D-shackle Part number RTC 7032.

Purpose-designed rope hooks and D-shackles (Part numbers RTC7031 and RTC 7032) are suitable for capstan and drum winches. The hook is used on Capstan winches as an integral part of the polypropylene rope (Part number RTC 7030) and on drum winches in conjunction with D-shackles (Part number RTC 7032). This D-shackle has been chosen because it can be passed through the eye of the hook, and the pin will pass through the eye terminations in the end of wire cables Part numbers RTC 7028, RTC 7029 and RTC 7040 (Extension Cable) used on drum winches.

POLYPROPYLENE CAPSTAN WINCH ROPES

Polypropylene Capstan Winch Ropes (Part number RTC 7030) are supplied in 50 feet coils ready for use; rotproof, resistant to attack from alkalis, acids and oils, with maximum rope extension of 44 per cent of original length.

Part number:

RTC 7030   Polypropylene Capstan Winch Rope

WIRE ROPE

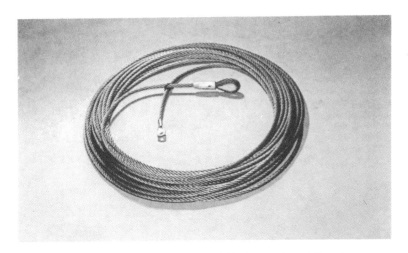

A range of high tensile wire ropes are available in a variety of diameters
and lengths to suit every winch in the Land Rover Parts Ltd. line up. All
winch ropes are individually certified.

Part number:

Wire Ropes	Diameter	Length	Winch Applications
RTC 7028	9.5mm	45.70mtr	RTC 8888 Mechanical Drum Winch
RTC 7029	9.5mm	30.50mtr	RTC 8013 Electrical Drum Winch
RTC 8885	8mm	24.00mtr	RTC 8881 8000lb Electric Winch
RTC 8884	6.4mm	30.00mtr	RTC 8880 5000lb Electric Winch

EXTENSION CABLE

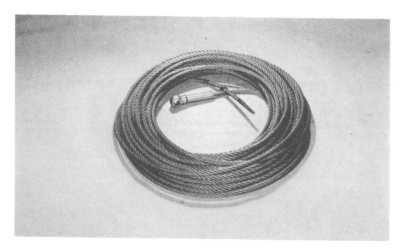

Extension cable Part number RTC 7040 for use with winches Part numbers RTC 8888 and RTC 8013 and pulley block RTC 7034.

NOTE: This extension cable must **NEVER** be drawn through the roller guides of the drum winch as it will damage the rollers, the winch cable and the cable end fittings. Likewise, the joint between the two cables must **NEVER** pass the pulley block RTC 7034 as it will severely damage cables, joints between the cables and the pulley block.

Extension cable (for use with winches Part numbers RTC 8888 and RTC 8013)

Part number

RTC 7040   Diameter 9.5mm Length 22.80mtr

PULLEY BLOCK FOR WIRE ROPES

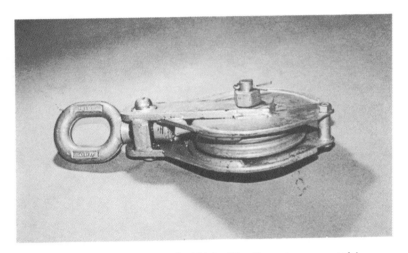

The Pulley Block Part number RTC 7034 for Wire Ropes is a very useful accessory and very simple to use. This pulley block is suitable for use with winch wire of 8mm or 9mm diameter and has a swivelling eye to prevent the winch cable twisting under load.

Part number

RTC 7034   Pulley Block for Wire Rope

TOW ROPE

Tow rope Part number RTC 8878 is a strong rope specially designed for vehicle towing. Made from buoyant "safety red" polypropylene, the rope is fitted with thimble eyes at each end which incorporate the attachment hooks. This method of termination substantially reduces stress at these points caused by "snatch" during a towing operation.

Specification

Rope Type   Safety Red Polypropylene

Rope diameter   24mm (15/16in)

Safe Working Load   1360kg (3000lbs)

Part number

RTC 8878   Polypropylene Tow Rope

VEHICLE ANCHORS

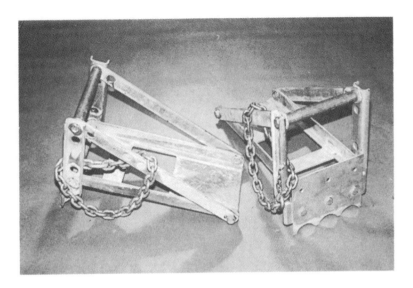

Vehicle Anchors Part number 583590 greatly increase the stability of the winching vehicle, are simple to use and extremely effective.

Once assembled, each anchor is placed in front of a vehicle's front wheels, setting the toothed blade according to ground condition, hard or soft. The vehicle is then driven onto the platform of the anchors until resistance to forward motion is felt. Before the vehicle rolls back naturally, apply the handbrake and hook the chains over the bumper, ensuring that they are as close to chassis side-members as possible.

N.B. When using vehicle anchors, to prevent transmission damage, manual or automatic transmissions should be placed in neutral.

TOWING AND LIFTING RINGS

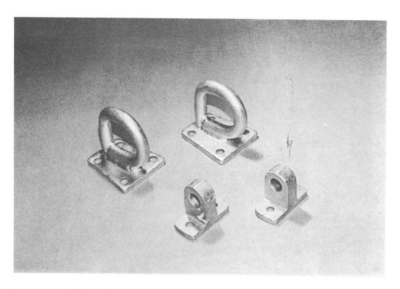

Towing and Lifting Rings can be fitted to all Land Rovers and provide the ideal anchor-point for rope or winch hook when conducting a double line-pull. They can also be used for attaching a rope to a vehicle where recovery operations do not warrant the use of a winch.

Part number

267950   Land Rover SIII — Towing and Lifting Ring

559882   Land Rover Ninety and One Ten — Towing and Lifting Ring (used in conjuction with D shackle RTC 7032).

The LAND ROVER 3.5 tonne Standard Towing Jaw

The Land Rover 3.5 tonne standard towing jaw is suitable for a wide winching application and can be affixed with a suitable fixing and bracing plate to either the front or rear of the vehicle, and is ideally suited for all types of winching and vehicle recovery use.

Part number

RTC 90518674   Standard Jaw 3.5 tonne.

Ground anchors of many types have been produced to overcome the problems of establishing an anchor in a variety of ground conditions. For practical winching purposes two types of ground anchor have been developed to cover a wide range of ground conditions from medium loams to firm ground containing large amounts of small stones. These are the MOLEX ground anchor from TIRFOR LTD., and the STAKED BAR ground anchor from BUSHEY HALL WINCHES AND EQUIPMENT LTD. Both these ground anchors are easily deployed and retrieved and when not in use take up little space in the parent vehicle.

THE MOLEX GROUND ANCHOR

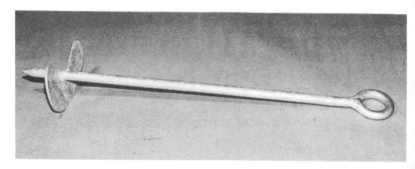

The MOLEX ground anchor from TIRFOR LTD. This very practical ground anchor is ideal for general winching use.

Available from:

Tirfor Limited, Holbrock Industrial Estate, Old Lane, Halfway, Sheffield, South Yorkshire S19 5GZ Tel: (0742) 482266, Telex 54354 TIRFOR G

THE STAKED BAR GROUND ANCHOR

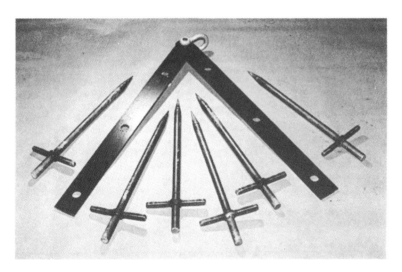

The STAKED BAR ground anchor from BUSHEY HALL WINCHES AND
EQUIPMENT LTD. is well suited to a large variety of ground conditions,
and is at its best in medium to heavy loams or ground containing small
stones. When properly deployed in firm ground it should withstand a pull
of around 2 tonnes.

Available from:

Bushey Hall Winches and Equipment Limited, Unit 7,

Lismirrane Industrial Park, Elstree Road,

Elstree, Borehamwood, Hertfordshire WD6 3EE

Tel: 01 – 953 6050 Fax: 01 – 207 5308

Conversion Formulae

To Convert	Multiply by	To Convert	Multiply by
Inches to Centimetres	2.540	Sq Metres to Sq Feet	10.763 9
Centimetres to Inches	0.393 701	Sq Feet to Sq Metres	0.092 903
Feet to Metres	0.304 8	Sq Yards to Sq Metres	0.836 127
Metres to Feet	3.280 8	Sq Metres to Sq Yards	1.195 99
Yards to Metres	0.914 4	Sq Miles to Sq Kilometres	2.589 99
Metres to Yards	1.093 61	Sq Kilometres to Sq Miles	0.386 103
Miles to Kilometres	1.609 34	Acres to Hectares	0.404 678
Kilometres to Miles	0.621 371	Hectares to Acres	2.471 01
Sq Inches to Sq C/metres	6.451 6	Cubic Ins to Cubic C/metres	16.387 1
Sq C/metres to Sq Inches	0.155 000	Cubic C/metres to Cubic Ins	0.061 023 7

Degrees Celcius (Centigrade) converted to Degrees Fahrenheit
Multiply °C by 9/5 and add 32

To Convert	Multiply by	To Convert	Multiply by
Cubic Feet to Cubic Metres	0.028 3168	Grams to Grains	15.43
Cubic Metres to Cubic Feet	35.314 7	Ounces to Grams	28.349 5
Cubic Yards to Cubic Metres	0.764 555	Grams to Ounces	0.035 274
Cubic Metres to Cubic Yards	1.307 95	Pounds to Grams	453.592
Cubic Inches to Litres	0.016 387	Grams to Pounds	0.002 204 62
Litres to Cubic Inches	61.024	Pounds to Kilograms	0.453 6
Gallons to Litres	4.546	Kilograms to Pounds	2.204 62
Litres to Gallons	0.22	Tons to Kilograms	1016.05
Grains to Grams	0.064 8	Kilograms to Tons	0.000 984 2

Degrees Fahrenheit converted to Degrees Celcius (Centigrade)
Multiply °F by 5/9 after subtracting 32

Weights and Measures

Apothecaries' Fluid Measure

		1 Minim	=	0.059 19 Millilitre
60 Minims	=	1 Fluid Drachm	=	3.552 Millilitres
8 Fluid Drachms	=	1 Fluid Ounce	=	28.413 Millilitres
20 Fluid Ounces	=	1 Imperial Pint	=	0.568 3 Litre
2 Pints	=	1 Quart	=	1.136 5 Litres
8 Pints	=	1 Gallon	=	4.546 1 Litres

Avoirdupois Weight

		1 Grain	=	0.064 8 Gramme
27.34375 Troy Grains	=	1 Dram	=	1.771 8 Grammes
16 Drams	=	1 Ounce	=	28.349 Grammes
16 Ounces	=	1 Pound	=	453.592 Grammes
14 Pounds	=	1 Stone	=	6.35 Kilogrammes
28 Pounds	=	1 Quarter	=	12.7 Kilogrammes
100 Pounds	=	1 Cental or New cwt	=	45.359 Kilogrammes
4 Qrs or 112 Pounds	=	1 Cwt	=	50.802 Killogrammes
20 Cwt	=	1 Ton	=	1016.05 Kilogrammes

Weights and Measures

Measures of Capacity for Liquids and Dry Goods

8.665 Cubic Inches	=	1 Gill	=	0.142 1 Litre
4 Gills	=	1 Pint	=	0.568 3 Litre
2 Pints	=	1 Quart	=	1.136 6 Litres
4 Quarts	=	1 Gallon	=	4.546 1 Litres
2 Gallons	=	1 Peck	=	9.092 2 Litres
4 Pecks	=	1 Bushel	=	36.368 Litres
8 Bushels	=	1 Quarter	=	2.909 5 Hectolitres
		1 Sq Inch	=	0.064 5 Sq Decim
144 Sq Inches	=	1 Sq Foot	=	9.290 3 Sq Decim
9 Sq Feet	=	1 Sq Yard	=	0.836 127 Sq Metre
1210 Sq Yards	=	1 Rood	=	10.117 1 Ares
4 Roods or 4840 Sq Yards	=	1 Acre	=	0.404 68 Hectare
640 Acres	=	1 Sq Miles	=	259.0 Hectares

95

Printed and distributed by Brooklands Books Ltd., P.O. Box 146, Cobham,
Surrey KT11 1LG, England Phone: 01932 865051 Fax: 01932 868803
E-mail: sales@brooklands-books.com   www.brooklands-books.com

ISBN 1 85520 2980   Part No. SMR 699MI   10/7Z6
        Printed in China   Ref: B-LRWHH

Road Test books on Land Rover and Range Rover

LAND ROVER
SERIES I-II & IIA
Gold Portfolio

1948-1971
80 • 86 • 107 • 88 • 109
Petrol and Diesel
4 and 6 cylinder

LAND ROVER
SERIES III
4 X 4 PERFORMANCE PORTFOLIO
1971-1985

Road tests   New model introductions   Performance data
Buying used   Touring   Specifications   Customising
Pick-up   Wagon   hard top   Safari   2 & 6 cyl   V8   Diesel

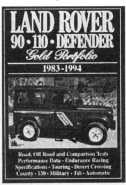

LAND ROVER
90 • 110 • DEFENDER
Gold Portfolio
1983-1994

Road, Off Road and Comparison Tests
Performance Data • Endurance Racing
Specifications • Touring • Desert Crossing
County • 130 • Military • Tdi • Automatic

Land Rover
DISCOVERY
4x4 PERFORMANCE PORTFOLIO
1989-2000

Road and comparison tests   Off road reports   Performance data
Buyers' guide   Model introductions and updates   Specifications
Petrol Mpi V8 3.5 3.9 & 4.0   Turbo diesel 200Tdi 300Tdi & Td5

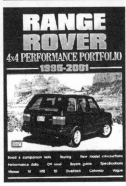

COMBAT
LAND ROVERS
LRM Portfolio No.1
by Bob Morrison

RANGE ROVER
Gold Portfolio
1970-1985

Road Tests • New Model Introductions
Long Term and Off Road Reports • Updates
Performance Data • History • Buying Used
Vogue • Janspeed • Schuler • Automatic

RANGE ROVER
Gold Portfolio
1985-1995

Road and comparison tests   Touring   Specifications
Technical and performance data   Model introductions
Long term reports   Janspeed Highline   Buying used
County Vogue Tdi EFi LSE SE CSK LWB

RANGE ROVER
4x4 PERFORMANCE PORTFOLIO
1995-2001

Road & comparison tests   Touring   New model introductions
Performance data   Off road   Buyers guide   Specifications
Vitesse   SE   HSE   TD   Overfinch   Callaway   Vogue

RANGE ROVER
TAKES ON THE COMPETITION

American, Australian and British experts compare the Range Rover
against the Jeep Cherokee Pioneer & Grand Wagoneer • Ford Bronco
Toyota Land Cruiser & Amazon • Mitsubishi Shogun • Isuzu Trooper
Lada Niva • Mercedes ML320 & G-Wagon • GMC Jimmy • Vauxhall
Monterey • Suzuki SJ • Lexus LX 450 • Lamborghini LM002 and many
more. Also included are road model reports, performance data
and specifications, plus advice on purchasing a used Range Rover

---

From specialist booksellers or, in case of difficulty, direct from the distributors:

Brooklands Books Ltd., PO Box 146, Cobham, Surrey, KT11 1LG, England. Phone: 01932 865051   Fax: 01932 868803
E-Mail: sales@brooklands-books.com www.brooklands-books.com
ɔklands Books Australia, 3/37-39 Green Street, Banksmeadow, NSW 2019, Australia. Phone: 2 9695 7055   Fax: 2 9695 7355
ɔarTech, 39966 Grand Avenue, North Branch, MN 55056, USA. Phone: 800 551 4754 & 651 277 1200   Fax: 651 277 1203

Brooklands Books

MOTORING

ROAD TEST SERIES
Abarth Gold Portfolio 1950-1971
Alta Romeo Giulietta Gold Portfolio 1954-1965
Alta Romeo Giulia Coupés 1963-1976
Alfa Romeo Spider 1966-1990
Alfa Romeo Alfasud 1972-1984
Alfa Romeo Alfetta Gold Portfolio 1972-1987
Alfa Romeo Spider & GTV Perf. Port. 1995-2005
Alvis Gold Portfolio 1919-1967
AMC Rambler Limited Edition Extra 1956-1969
AMX & Javelin Gold Portfolio 1968-1974
Armstrong Siddeley Gold Portfolio 1945-1960
Aston Martin Gold Portfolio 1921-1947
Aston Martin Ultimate Portfolio 1948-1968
Aston Martin Ultimate Portfolio 1968-1980
Aston Martin Ultimate Portfolio 1981-1993
Aston Martin Ultimate Portfolio 1994-2006
Audi Quattro Gold Portfolio 1980-1991
Audi Quattro Takes On The Competition
Audi TT Performance Portfolio 1998-2006
Austin-Healey 100 & 100/6 Gold Port. 1952-1959
Austin-Healey 3000 Ultimate Portfolio 1959-1967
Austin-Healey Sprite Gold Portfolio 1958-1971
Bentley & Rolls-Royce Portfolio 1990-2002
Berkeley Sportscars Limited Edition
BMW 6 & 8 Cyl. Cars Limited Edition 1935-1960
BMW 700 Limited Edition 1959-1965
BMW 1600 Collection No. 1 1966-1981
BMW 2002 Ultimate Portfolio
BMW 6 Cylinder Coupés & Saloons Gold P. 1969-1976
BMW 316, 318, 320 (4 cyl.) Gold Port. 1975-1990
BMW 320, 323, 325 (6 cyl.) Gold Port. 1977-1990
BMW 3 Series Gold Portfolio 1991-1997
BMW 5 Series Gold Portfolio 1988-1995
BMW 6 Series Ultimate Portfolio 1976-1989
BMW 7 Series Performance Portfolio 1977-1986
BMW 7 Series Performance Portfolio 1986-1993
BMW 8 Series Performance Portfolio
BMW Alpina Performance Portfolio 1967-1987
BMW Alpina Performance Portfolio 1988-1998
BMW Z3, M Coupe & M Roadster Gold Port. 1996-02
Borgward Isabella Limited Edition
Bristol Cars Portfolio
Buick Performance Portfolio 1947-1962
Buick Muscle Portfolio 1963-1973
Buick Riviera Performance Portfolio 1963-1978
Cadillac Performance Portfolio 1948-1958
Cadillac Performance Portfolio 1959-1966
Cadillac Eldorado Performance Portfolio 1967-1978
Cadillac Allante Limited Edition Extra
Chevrolet 1955-1957
Impala & SS Muscle Portfolio 1958-1972
Corvair Performance Portfolio 1959-1969
El Camino & SS Muscle Portfolio 1959-1987
Chevy II & Nova SS Gold Portfolio 1962-1974
Chevelle & SS Gold Portfolio 1964-1972
Camaro Muscle Portfolio 1967-1973
Camaro Performance Portfolio 1993-2000
Chevrolet Corvette Gold Portfolio 1953-1962
Chevrolet Corvette Sting Ray Gold Port. 1963-1967
Chevrolet Corvette Gold Portfolio 1968-1977
High Performance Corvettes 1983-1989
Chrysler Imperial Gold Portfolio 1951-1975
Valiant 1960-1962
PT Cruiser Performance Portfolio
Citroen 2CV Ultimate Portfolio 1948-1990
Citroen DS & ID 1955-1975
Citroen DS & ID Gold Portfolio 1955-1975
Citroen SM Limited Edition Extra 1970-1975
Shelby Cobra Gold Portfolio 1962-1969
Crosley & Crosley Specials Limited Edition
Cunningham Automobiles 1951-1955
Datsun Roadsters Performance Portfolio 1960-71
Datsun 240Z & 260Z Gold Portfolio 1970-1978
DeLorean Gold Portfolio 1977-1995
De Soto Limited Edition 1952-1960
Dodge Limited Edition 1949-1959
Dodge Dart Limited Edition Extra 1960-1976
Dodge Muscle Portfolio 1964-1971
Charger Muscle Portfolio 1966-1974
ERA Gold Portfolio 1934-1994
Facel Vega Limited Edition Extra 1954-1964
Ferrari Limited Edition 1947-1957
Ferrari Limited Edition 1958-1963
Ferrari Dino Limited Edition Extra 1965-1974
Ferrari 328 348 Mondial Ultimate Portfolio 1986-94
Ferrari F355 & 360 Gold Portfolio 1995-2004
Fiat 600 & 850 Gold Portfolio 1955-1972
Fiat Dino Limited Edition
Fiat X1/9 Gold Portfolio 1973-1989
Ford Consul, Zephyr, Zodiac Mk. I & II 1950-1962
Ford Zephyr, Zodiac, Executive Mk. III & IV 1962-1971
High Performance Capris Gold Portfolio 1969-1987
Capri Muscle Portfolio 1974-1987
High Performance Fiestas 1979-1991
Ford Escort RS & Mexico Limited Edition 1970-1979
High Performance Escorts Mk. II 1975-1980
High Performance Escorts 1980-1985
High Performance Escorts 1985-1990
Ford Thunderbird Performance Portfolio 1955-1957
Ford Thunderbird Performance Portfolio 1958-1963
Ford Thunderbird Performance Portfolio 1964-1976
Ford Fairlane Performance Portfolio 1955-1970
Ford Ranchero Muscle Portfolio 1957-1979
Edsel Limited Edition 1957-1960
Ford Galaxie & LTD Gold Portfolio 1960-1976
Falcon Performance Portfolio 1960-1970
Ford Torino Performance Portfolio 1968-1974
Ford Bronco 4x4 Performance Portfolio 1966-1977
Ford Bronco 1978-1988
Shelby Mustang Ultimate Portfolio 1965-1970
Mustang Muscle Portfolio 1967-1973
High Performance Mustang IIs 1974-1978
Mustang 5.0L Muscle Portfolio 1982-1993
Mustang 5.0L Takes On The Competition
Goggomobil Limited Edition
Holden 1948-1962
Honda S500 • S600 • S800 Limited Edition 1962-1970
Honda CRX 1983-1987
Hudson Performance Portfolio 1946-1957
International Scout Gold Portfolio 1961-1980
Isetta Gold Portfolio 1953-1964
Jaguar and SS Gold Portfolio 1931-1951
Jaguar C-Type & D-Type Gold Portfolio 1951-1960
Jaguar XK120, 140, 150 Gold Portfolio 1948-1960
Jaguar Mk. VII, VIII, IX, X, 420 Gold Port. 1950-1970
Jaguar E-Type Gold Portfolio 1961-1971
Jaguar XJ6 Series I & II Gold Portfolio 1968-1979
Jaguar XJ6 Series III Perf. Portfolio 1979-1986
Jaguar XJS Gold Portfolio 1975-1988
Jaguar XJ-S V12 Ultimate Portfolio 1988-1996
Jaguar XK8 Limited Edition
Jeep CJ-5 Limited Edition 1960-1975
Jeep CJ-5 & CJ-7 4x4 Perf. Portfolio 1976-1986
Jeep Wagoneer Performance Portfolio 1963-1991
Jeep J-Series Pickups 1970-1982
Jeepster & Commando Limited Edition 1967-1973
Jeep Cherokee & Comanche Pickups P. P. 1984-91
Jeep Wrangler 4x4 Performance Portfolio 1987-99
Jeep Cherokee & Grand Cherokee 4x4 P. P. 1992-98
Jensen Interceptor Ultimate Portfolio 1966-1992
Jensen - Healey Limited Edition 1972-1976
Kaiser - Frazer Limited Edition 1946-1955
Lagonda Gold Portfolio 1919-1964
Lancia Aurelia & Flaminia Gold Portfolio 1950-1970
Lancia Fulvia Gold Portfolio 1963-1976
Lancia Beta Gold Portfolio 1972-1984
Lancia Stratos Limited Edition Extra
Lancia Delta & integrale Ultimate Portfolio
Land Rover Series I, II & IIA Gold Portfolio 1948-71
Land Rover Series III 4x4 Perf. Portfolio 1971-1985
Land Rover 90 110 Defender Gold Portfolio 1983-94
Land Rover Discovery Perf. Port. 1989-2000
Fifty Years of Selling Land Rover
Lamboghini Performance Portfolio 1964-1976
Lamboghini Performance Portfolio 1977-1989
Lamboghini Gold Portfolio 1990-2004
Lincoln Gold Portfolio 1949-1960
Lincoln Continental Performance Portfolio 1961-1969
Lincoln Continental 1969-1976
Lotus Sports Racers Portfolio - covering 1951-1965
Lotus Seven Gold Portfolio 1957-1973
Lotus Elite Limited Edition 1957-1964
Lotus Elan Ultimate Portfolio 1962-1974
Lotus Elan & SE 1989-1992
Lotus Europa Gold Portfolio 1966-1975
Lotus Elite & Eclat 1974-1982
Lotus Elise & Exige Gold Portfolio 1995-2005
Marcos Coupés & Spyders Gold Portfolio 1960-1997
Maserati Cars Performance Portfolio 1957-1970
Maserati Cars Performance Portfolio 1971-1982
Maserati Cars Performance Portfolio 1982-1998
Matra Limited Edition 1965-1983
Mazda Miata MX-5 Performance Portfolio 1989-1997
Mazda Miata MX-5 Performance Portfolio 1998-2005
Mazda Miata MX-5 Takes On The Competition
Mazda RX-7 Gold Portfolio 1978-1991
McLaren F1 • GTR • LM Sportscar Perf. Portfolio
Mercedes 190 & 300 SL 1954-1963
Mercedes S & 600 Limited Edition Extra 1965-1972
Mercedes S Class 1972-1979
Mercedes S Class Limited Edition Extra 1980-1991
Mercedes 230 • 250 • 280SL Gold Portfolio 1963-1971
Mercedes-Benz SLs & SLCs Ultimate Port. 1971-89
Mercedes SLs Performance Portfolio 1989-1994
Mercedes G-Wagen Gold Portfolio 1981-2005
Mercedes 190 Limited Edition Extra 1983-1993
Mercedes CLK & SLK Limited Edition
Mercury Gold Portfolio 1947-1966
Mercury Comet & Cyclone Lim. Edit. Extra 1960-75
Cougar Muscle Portfolio 1967-1973
Messerschmitt Gold Portfolio 1954-1964
MG Gold Portfolio 1929-1939
MG TA & TC Gold Portfolio 1936-1949
MG TD & TF Gold Portfolio 1949-1955
MGA & Twin Cam Gold Portfolio 1955-1962
MG Midget Gold Portfolio 1961-1979
MGB Roadsters 1962-1980
MGB MGC & V8 Gold Portfolio 1962-1980
MGC & MGB GT V8 Limited Edition
MGF & TF Performance Portfolio 1995-2005
Mini Gold Portfolio 1959-1969
Mini Gold Portfolio 1969-1980
Mini Gold Portfolio 1981-1997
High Performance Minis Gold Portfolio 1960-1973
Mini Cooper Gold Portfolio 1961-1971
Mini Moke Ultimate Portfolio 1964-1994
Mini Performance Portfolio 2001-2006
Starion & Conquest Performance Portfolio 1982-90
Mitsubishi 3000GT & Dodge Stealth P.P. 1990-99
Morgan Three-Wheeler Gold Portfolio 1910-1952
Morgan Plus 4 & Four 4 Gold Portfolio 1936-1967
Morgan Cars Portfolio 1968-2001
Morris Minor Collection No. 1 1948-1980
Nash Limited Edition Extra 1949-1957
Nash-Austin Metropolitan Gold Portfolio 1954-1962
Nissan Skyliner GT-R Limited Edition Extra 1989-02
NSU Ro80 Limited Edition
NSX Performance Portfolio 1989-1999
Oldsmobile Automobiles 1955-1963
Oldsmobile Muscle Portfolio 1964-1971
Cutlass & 4-4-2 Muscle Portfolio 1964-1974
Opel GT Ultimate Portfolio 1968-1973
Opel Manta Limited Edition 1970-1975
Pantera Ultimate Portfolio 1970-1995
Panther Gold Portfolio 1972-1990
Plymouth Limited Edition 1950-1960
Plymouth Fury Limited Edition Extra 1956-1976
Barracuda Muscle Portfolio 1964-1974
Plymouth Muscle Portfolio 1964-1971
High Performance Firebirds 1982-1988
Firebird & Trans Am Performance Portfolio 1993-00
Pontiac Fiero Performance Portfolio 1984-1988
Pursche Sports Racers Ultimate Portfolio 1952-1968
Porsche 917 • 935 • 956 • 962 Sports Racers Gold Port.
Porsche 912 Limited Edition Extra
Porsche 365 Ultimate Portfolio 1952-1965
Porsche 911 1965-1969
Porsche 911 1973-1977
Porsche 911 SC & Turbo Gold Portfolio 1978-1983
Porsche 911 Carrera & Turbo Gold Port. 1984-1989
Porsche 911 Ultimate Portfolio 1990-1997
Porsche 911 Takes On The Competition 1990-1997
Porsche 911 Ultimate Portfolio 1998-2004
Porsche 914 Ultimate Portfolio
Porsche 924 Gold Portfolio 1975-1988
Porsche 928 Gold Portfolio 1977-1995
Porsche 928 Takes On The Competition
Porsche 944 Ultimate Portfolio
Porsche 968 Limited Edition Extra
Porsche Boxster Ultimate Portfolio 1996-2004
Railton & Brough Superior Gold Portfolio 1933-1950
Range Rover Gold Portfolio 1970-1985
Range Rover Gold Portfolio 1985-1995
Range Rover Performance Portfolio 1995-2001
Range Rover Takes on the Competition
Riley Gold Portfolio 1924-1939
Rolls-Royce Silver Clould & Bentley S Ultimate Port.
Rolls-Royce Silver Shadow Ultimate Port. 1965-80
Rolls-Royce & Bentley Gold Portfolio 1980-1989
Rover P4 1949-1959
Rover 2000 & 2200 1963-1977
Subaru Impreza Turbo Limited Edition Extra 94-00
Subaru Impreza WRX Performance Port. 2001-05
Studebaker Hawks & Larks 1956-1963
Avanti Limited Edition Extra 1962-1991
Sunbeam Alpine Limited Edition Extra 1959-1968
Sunbeam Tiger Limited Edition Extra 1964-1967
Suzuki SJ Gold Portfolio 1971-1997
Vitara, Sidekick & Geo Tracker Perf. Port. 1988-1997
Toyota Land Cruiser Gold Portfolio 1956-1987
Toyota Land Cruiser 1988-1997
Toyota Supra Performance Portfolio 1982-1998
Toyota MR2 Gold Portfolio 1984-1997
Toyota MR2 Takes On The Competition
Triumph TR2 & TR3 Gold Portfolio 1952-1961
Triumph TR4, TR5, TR250 1961-1968
Triumph TR6 Gold Portfolio 1969-1976
Triumph Herald 1959-1971
Triumph Vitesse 1962-1971
Triumph Spitfire Gold Portfolio 1962-1980
Triumph 2000, 2.5, 2500 1963-1977
Triumph GT6 Gold Portfolio 1966-1974
Triumph Stag Gold Portfolio 1970-1977
Triumph Dolomite Sprint Limited Edition
TVR Gold Portfolio 1959-1986
TVR Performance Portfolio 1986-1994
TVR Performance Portfolio 1995-2000
TVR Performance Portfolio 2000-2005
VW Beetle Gold Portfolio 1935-1967
VW Beetle Gold Portfolio 1968-1991
VW Bus, Camper, Van Perf. Portfolio 1954-1967
VW Bus, Camper, Van Perf. Portfolio 1968-1979
VW Bus, Camper, Van Perf. Portfolio 1979-1991
VW Karmann Ghia Gold Portfolio 1955-1974
VW Scirocco 1974-1981
VW Golf GTI Limited Edition Extra 1976-1991
VW Corrado Limited Edition 1989-1995
Volvo PV444 & PV544 Perf. Portfolio 1945-1965
Volvo 120 Amazon Ultimate Portfolio
Volvo 1800 Ultimate Portfolio 1960-1973
Volvo 140 & 160 Series Gold Portfolio 1966-1975
Forty Years of Selling Volvo
Westfield Performance Portfolio 1982-2004

CAR AND DRIVER SERIES
Car and Driver on BMW 1957-1977
Car and Driver on Corvette 1978-1982
Car and Driver on Corvette 1983-1988
Car and Driver on Ferrari 1955-1962
Car and Driver on Ferrari 1963-1975
Car and Driver on Mopar 1956-1967
Car and Driver on Mustang 1964-1973
Car and Driver on Porsche 1955-1962
Car and Driver on Porsche 1963-1970
Car and Driver on Porsche 1970-1976
Car and Driver on Porsche 1977-1981
Car and Driver on Porsche 1982-1986

RACING & THE LAND SPEED RECORD
The Land Speed Record 1898-1919
The Land Speed Record 1920-1929
The Land Speed Record 1930-1939
The Land Speed Record 1940-1962
The Land Speed Record 1963-1999
Can-Am Racing 1966-1969
Can-Am Racing 1970-1974
Can-Am Racing Cars 1966-1974
The Carrera Panamericana Mexico - 1950-1954
Le Mans - The Bentley & Alfa Years - 1923-1939
Le Mans - The Jaguar Years - 1949-1957
Le Mans - The Ferrari Years - 1958-1965
Le Mans - The Ford & Matra Years - 1966-1974
Le Mans - The Porsche Years - 1975-1982
Le Mans - The Porsche & Jaguar Years - 1983-91
Le Mans - The Porsche & Peugeot Years - 1992-99
Mille Miglia - The Alfa & Ferrari Years - 1927-1951
Mille Miglia - The Ferrari & Mercedes Years - 1952-57
Targa Florio - The Porsche & Ferrari Years - 1955-1964
Targa Florio - The Porsche Years - 1965-1973

ROAD & TRACK 'PORTFOLIO' SERIES
Road & Track BMW M Series Portfolio 1979-2002
R & T BMW Z3, M Coupe & M Roadster Port. 96-02
R & T Camaro & Firebird Portfolio 1993-2002
Road & Track Corvette Portfolio 1997-2002
Road & Track Dodge Viper Portfolio 1992-2002
Road & Track Ferrari V-12 Portfolio 1992-2002
Road & Track Ferrari F355 360 F430 Portfolio 95-06
R & T Jaguar XJ-S - XK8 - XKR Portfolio 1975-2003
R & T Mercedes SL - SLK - CLK Portfolio 1990-03
Road & Track MX-5 Miata Portfolio 1989-2002
Road & Track Mustang Portfolio 1994-2002
Road & Track Nissan 300ZX & 350Z Portfolio 1984
Road & Track Porsche 928 Portfolio 1977-1994
Road & Track Porsche 911 Portfolio 1990-1997

ROAD & TRACK 'ON' SERIES
Road & Track on Aston Martin 1962-1990
Road & Track on Audi & Auto Union 1952-1980
Road & Track on Audi & Auto Union 1980-1986
Road & Track on Austin Healey 1953-1970
Road & Track on BMW Cars 1966-1974
Road & Track on BMW Cars 1975-1978
Road & Track on BMW Cars 1979-1983
R & T on Cobra, Shelby & Ford GT40 1962-1992
Road & Track on Corvette 1968-1982
Road & Track on Corvette 1982-1986
Road & Track on Corvette 1986-1990
Road & Track on Ferrari 1975-1981
Road & Track on Ferrari 1981-1984
Road & Track on Ferrari 1984-1988
Road & Track on Fiat Sports Cars 1968-1987
Road & Track on Jaguar 1950-1960
Road & Track on Jaguar 1961-1968
Road & Track on Jaguar 1968-1974
Road & Track on Jaguar 1974-1982
Road & Track on Jaguar 1983-1989
Road & Track on Lamborghini 1964-1985
Road & Track on Mercedes 1952-1962
Road & Track on Mercedes 1963-1970
Road & Track on Mercedes 1971-1979
Road & Track on MG Sports Cars 1949-1961
Road & Track on MG Sports Cars 1962-1980
Road & Track on Pontiac 1960-1983
Road & Track on Porsche 1951-1967
Road & Track on Porsche 1968-1971
Road & Track on Porsche 1972-1975
Road & Track on Porsche 1975-1978
Road & Track on Porsche 1979-1982
Road & Track on Porsche 1985-1988
R & T on Rolls Royce & Bentley 1950-1965
R & T on Rolls Royce & Bentley 1966-1984
Road & Track on Saab 1972-1992
R & T on Toyota Sports & GT Cars 1966-1984
R & T on Triumph Sports Cars 1967-1974
R & T on Triumph Sports Cars 1974-1982
Road & Track on Volkswagen 1951-1968
Road & Track on Volkswagen 1968-1978
Road & Track on Volkswagen 1978-1985
Road & Track on Volvo 1957-1974
Road & Track on Volvo 1977-1994

ROAD & TRACK BY AUTHOR
Road & Track - Henry Manney at Large & Abroad
Road & Track - Best of PS
Road & Track - Peter Egan Side Glances 1983-92
Road & Track - Peter Egan Side Glances 1992-97
Road & Track - Peter Egan Side Glances 1998-02
Road & Track - Peter Egan Side Glances 2002-06

PRACTICAL CLASSICS SERIES
PC on Midget/Sprite Restoration
PC on MGB Restoration
PC on Sunbeam Rapier Restoration

HOT ROD 'ENGINE' SERIES
Chevy 265 & 283
Chevy 302 & 327
Chevy 348 & 409
Chevy 396 & 427
Chevy 454 thru 512
Chrysler Hemi
Chrysler 273, 318, 340 & 360
Chrysler 361, 383, 400, 413, 426 & 440
Ford 289, 302, Boss 302 & 351W
Ford 351C & Boss 351
Ford Big Block

RESTORATION & GUIDE SERIES
BMW 2002 - A Comprehensive Guide
BMW '02 Restoration Guide
BMW E30 - 3 Series Restoration Bible
Classic Camaro Restoration
Chevrolet High Performance Tips & Techniques
Engine Swapping Tips & Techniques
Land Rover Restoration Portfolio
Lotus Elan Restoration Guide
MG 'T' Series Restoration Guide
MGA Restoration Guide
Mustang Restoration Tips & Techniques
Practical Gas Flow
Restoring Sprites & Midgets an Enthusiast's Guide
SU Carburetters Tuning Tips & Techniques
The Great Classic Muscle Cars Compared

MILITARY VEHICLES
Complete WW2 Military Jeep Manual
Dodge WW2 Military Portfolio 1940-1945
German Military Equipment WW2
Hail To The Jeep
Combat Land Rover Portfolio No. 1
Land Rover Military Portfolio
Military & Civilian Amphibians 1940-1990
Off Road Jeeps Civilian & Military 1944-1971
US Military Vehicles 1941-1945
Standard Military Motor Vehicles-TM9-2800 (WW2)
VW Kubelwagen Military Portfolio 1940-1990
WW2 Allied Vehicles Military Portfolio 1939-1945
WW2 Jeep Military Portfolio 1941-1945

MOTORCYCLES
To see our range of over 60 titles visit
www.brooklands-books.com

WORKING IN THE WILD
LAND ROVER'S MANUAL FOR AFRICA

This book is designed to equip the Land Rover user with the practical know-how to make the most of the vehicle's capacity for hard work in hostile conditions. It looks at every stage in the working life of a Land Rover, selection, purchasing and how to drive it to maximum effect. A new section has been included to expand driving techniques and tyre choices. There are sections on unconventional workshops and how to avoid problems and overcome difficulties. The book is based on in-depth experience of Land Rover engineers and users over many years.

230 pages, 500 illus. Soft bound. Ref. B-LRAHH ISBN 185520 2859

www.brooklands-books.com

LAND ROVER OFFICIAL FACTORY PUBLICATIONS

Land Rover Series 1 Workshop Manual	4291
Land Rover Series 1 1948-53 Parts Catalogue	4051
Land Rover Series 1 1954-58 Parts Catalogue	4107
Land Rover Series 1 Instruction Manual	4277
Land Rover Series 1 & II Diesel Instruction Manual	4343
Land Rover Series II & IIA Workshop Manual	AKM8159
Land Rover Series II & Early IIA Bonneted Control Parts Catalogue	605957
Land Rover Series IIA Bonneted Control Parts Catalogue	RTC9840CC
Land Rover Series IIA, III & 109 V8 Optional Equipment Parts Catalogue	RTC9842CE
Land Rover Series IIA/IIB Instruction Manual	LSM64 IM
Land Rover Series III Workshop Manual	AKM3648
Land Rover Series III Workshop Manual V8 Supplement (edn. 2)	AKM8022
Land Rover Series III 88, 109 & 109 V8 Parts Catalogue	RTC9841CE
Land Rover Series III Owners' Manual 1971-81	607324B
Land Rover Series III Owners' Manual 1981-85	AKM8155
Land Rover 90/110 & Defender Workshop Manual 1983-92	SLR621ENWM
Land Rover Defender Workshop Manual 1993-95	LDAWMEN93
(Covering petrol 2.25, 2.5, 3.5 V8 & diesel 2.25, 2.5, 2.5 Turbo, 200 Tdi)	
Land Rover Defender 300 Tdi Workshop Manual 1996-98	LRL 0097 ENG
Land Rover Defender Td5 Workshop Manual & Supplements 1999-2005 on	LRL 0410BB
Land Rover Defender Electrical Manual Td5 99-05 on & 300Tdi 02-05 on	LRD5EHBB
Contains YVB 101670, VDL 100170, LRL 0452 ENG & LRL 0389 ENG	
Land Rover 110 Parts Catalogue 1983-86	RTC9863CE
Land Rover Defender Parts Catalogue 1987-2001 on	STC9021CC
Land Rover 90 • 110 Owners' Handbook 1983-1990	LSM0054
Land Rover 90 • 110 • 130 Owners' Handbook 1991-Feb. 1994	LHAHBEN93
Land Rover 90 • 110 • 130 Owners' Handbook March 1994-1998	LRL0087ENG/2
Discovery Workshop Manual 1990-94 (petrol 3.5, 3.9, Mpi & diesel 200 Tdi)	SJR900ENWM
Discovery Workshop Manual 1995-98 (petrol 2.0 Mpi, 3.9, 4.0 V8 & diesel 300 Tdi)	LRL0079
Discovery Series II Workshop Manual 1999-02 (petrol 4.0 V8 & diesel Td5)	VDR 100090
Discovery Parts Catalogue 1989-98 (2.0 Mpi, 3.5, 3.9 V8 & 200 Tdi & 300 Tdi)	RTC9947CF
Discovery Owners' Handbook 1990-1991 (petrol 3.5 & diesel 200 Tdi)	SJR820ENHB90
Freelander Workshop Manual 1998-2000 (petrol 1.8 and diesel 2.0)	LRL0144
Land Rover Military (Lightweight) Series III Parts Catalogue	
Land Rover Military (Lightweight) Series III User Manual	608180
Land Rover 101 1 Tonne Forward Control Workshop Manual	RTC9120
Land Rover 101 1 Tonne Forward Control Parts Catalogue	608294B
Land Rover 101 1 Tonne Forward Control User Manual	608239
Range Rover Workshop Manual 1970-85 (petrol 3.5)	AKM3630
Range Rover Workshop Manual 1986-89	SRR660ENWM &
(petrol 3.5 & diesel 2.4 Turbo VM & 2.5 Turbo VM)	LSM180WS4 Ed 2
Range Rover Workshop Manual 1990-94	
(petrol 3.9, 4.2 & diesel 2.5 Turbo VM, 200 Tdi)	LHAWMENA02
Range Rover Workshop Manual 1995-01 (petrol 4.0, 4.6 & BMW 2.5 diesel)	VDR 100370
Range Rover Parts Catalogue 1970-85 (petrol 3.5)	RTC9846CH
Range Rover Parts Catalogue 1986-91	
(petrol 3.5, 3.9 & diesel 2.4 Turbo VM & 2.5 Turbo VM)	RTC9908CB
Range Rover Parts Catalogue 1992-94 MY & 95 MY Classic	
(petrol 3.9, 4.2 & diesel 2.5 Turbo VM, 200 Tdi & 300 Tdi)	RTC9961CB
Range Rover Owners' Handbook 1970-80 (petrol 3.5)	606917
Range Rover Owners' Handbook 1981-82 (petrol 3.5)	AKM 8139
Range Rover Owners' Handbook 1983-85 (petrol 3.5)	LSM 0001HB
Range Rover Owners' Handbook 1986-87 (petrol 3.5 & diesel 2.4 Turbo VM)	LSM 129HB
Range Rover Owners' Handbook 1988-89 (petrol 3.5 & diesel 2.4 Turbo VM)	SRR600ENHB

Engine Overhaul Manuals for Land Rover & Range Rover

300 Tdi Engine, R380 Manual Gearbox & LT230T Transfer Gearbox Overhaul Manuals	LRL 003, 070 & 081
Petrol Engine V8 3.5, 3.9, 4.0, 4.2 & 4.6 Overhaul Manuals	LRL 004 & 164
Land Rover/Range Rover Driving Techniques	LR 369
Working in the Wild - Manual for Africa	SMR 684MI
Winching in Safety	SMR 699MI

Owners' Workhop Manuals
Land Rover 2 / 2A / 3 1959-1983 Owners' Workshop Manual
Land Rover 90, 110 & Defender 1983-1995 Owners' Workshop Manual

From Land Rover specialists or, in case of difficulty, direct from the distributors:
Brooklands Books Ltd., PO Box 146, Cobham, Surrey, KT11 1LG, England.
Telephone: 01932 865051 Fax: 01932 868803
e-mail sales@brooklands-books.com   www.brooklands-books.com
Brooklands Books Australia, 3/37-39 Green Street, Banksmeadow, NSW 2019, Australia
Phone: 2 9695 7055   Fax: 2 9695 7355
Car Tech, 39966 Grand Avenue, North Branch, MN 55056, USA
Telephone: 800 551 4754 & 651 277 1200 Fax: 651 277 1203